"Nathan Gardels and Nicolas Berggruen's insights into how we can restore individual economic security and rejuvenate deliberative democracy deserve the attention of every thoughtful citizen."

—Amy Gutmann, President, The University of Pennsylvania

"Aims to reconcile the power of direct participation with the equally necessary values of deliberation, pluralism, and compromise."

—Reid Hoffman, cofounder of LinkedIn

"Brilliantly explains our contemporary quandaries, proposes bold solutions, and lays down the foundations for reinventing good governance. A must-read for all—citizens and experts."

—Kishore Mahbubani, National University of Singapore, founding Dean of the Lee Kuan Yew School of Public Policy, author of *Has the West Lost It?*

"This book is a call for intellectual and emotional engagement in reshaping the governance of the world we live in."

—Fernando Henrique Cardoso, President of Brazil, 1995–2003

"A well-crafted case for rethinking globalism, nationalism, capitalism, and the appropriate forms of governance for the contemporary era, with a real sensitivity to wealth distribution and inequality."

—Margaret Levi, Sara Miller McCune Director, Center for Advanced Study in the Behavioral Sciences, Stanford University

"This incisively written volume pushes the boundaries of our understanding of the worldwide assault on democracy."

—Jonathan Aronson, Professor of Communications and Journalism, University of California, School of International Relations

"Gardels and Berggruen's blueprint for a sustainable future is essential material for the much-needed global deliberation required to find justice and harmony in this new stage of human history."

—Manuel Castells, Professor Emeritus of Sociology, University of California, Berkeley

Renovating Democracy

GREAT TRANSFORMATIONS

Craig Calhoun and Nils Gilman, Series Editors

Renovating Democracy

*Governing in the Age of
Globalization and Digital
Capitalism*

Nathan Gardels
and Nicolas Berggruen

UNIVERSITY OF CALIFORNIA PRESS

B **Berggruen**
Institute

University of California Press, one of the most distin-
guished university presses in the United States, enriches
lives around the world by advancing scholarship in the
humanities, social sciences, and natural sciences. Its
activities are supported by the UC Press Foundation and
by philanthropic contributions from individuals and
institutions. For more information, visit www.ucpress.edu.

University of California Press
Oakland, California

© 2019 by Nathan Gardels and Nicolas Berggruen

Library of Congress Cataloging-in-Publication Data

Names: Gardels, Nathan, author. | Berggruen, Nicolas,
   1961- author.
Title: Renovating democracy : governing in the age of
   globalization and digital capitalism / Nathan Gardels,
   Nicolas Berggruen.
Description: Oakland, California : University of
   California Press, [2019] | Includes bibliographical
   references and index. |
Identifiers: LCCN 2018033724 (print) | LCCN 2018036817
   (ebook) | ISBN 9780520972766 (ebook) |
   ISBN 9780520303607 (cloth : alk. paper)
Subjects: LCSH: United States—Politics and
   government—2017- | Democracy. | Capitalism. |
   Globalization.
Classification: LCC E912 (ebook) | LCC E912 .G36 2019 (print) |
   DDC 320.97309/0512—dc23
LC record available at https://lccn.loc.gov/2018033724

Manufactured in the United States of America

28 27 26 25 24 23 22 21 20 19
10 9 8 7 6 5 4 3 2 1

CONTENTS

There Is Something Wrong
with the System

The two of us, one an investor and the other a journalist and editor of an intellectual quarterly, had traversed the planet for decades and landed in Southern California, yet our paths had never crossed. That was until a casual introduction in 2010 by a mutual friend, Jacques Attali, the polymath futurist whom Francois Mitterrand called his "personal computer" when Attali was chief adviser to the late French president in the 1980s.

Like our French connection, we were worried about where our society was headed. Our shared sense that a world that had once worked was now broken bonded us like Felix and Oscar in *The Odd Couple*. In the opening scene of that great film starring Jack Lemmon and Walter Matthau, Felix asks Oscar, who is stomping around the apartment, why he is so upset. Oscar replies, "There is something wrong with the system, that's what's wrong."

We sat together for long discussions in Los Angeles that year, puzzling over what had gone so wrong with our adopted home state. California had long been the bellwether of America's bright future, where citizens dreamt of building a society equal to the magnificent landscape. Yet Californians at the early turn of the twenty-first century had settled instead for mountains of debt, D+ schools, public spending on prisons greater than on higher education, and an outdated, crumbling infrastructure. Because of partisan gridlock, the state legislature couldn't even produce a budget. State workers were paid with IOUs. In the years since the Beach Boys, the Mamas & the Papas, Joni Mitchell, and the Eagles had sung their globally resonant hymns about this culturally open, sunny frontier of the times ahead, it had all stalled, or even gone backward.

Having traveled extensively in Asia, we were both keenly aware that, during the same decades, poor little Singapore had risen from a Third World to a First World country. And that China, astonishingly, had lifted hundreds of millions out of destitution and built megacities with state-of-the-art subways and some of the world's tallest skyscrapers rising up into the clouds like calling cards of the new century. Was there a way to adapt some of their best practices of effective governance to our democratic values and individualistic, free-wheeling ways? That inquiry launched us on a journey of both theory and practice that has led to these present reflections.[1]

What concerned us most was that, as the public sphere so appallingly withered, the new global epicenter of creativity, innovation, and vast wealth creation was flourishing in Silicon Valley. It was just up the road from Salinas, where immigrant farmworkers were still to be seen bending their backs in a setting not far removed from the days described in John Steinbeck's *The Grapes of Wrath*. Google had been founded a little over a decade earlier; Facebook and Twitter a few years later. Much more was in the pipeline. Elon Musk's inventions were taking shape on the drawing board. Snapchat's Evan Spiegel, then only twenty, hadn't yet dropped out of Stanford to start what would become a company worth tens of billions, but his ideas were percolating. Down near San Diego, genetic pioneer Craig Venter was just setting up labs to advance the reading and rewriting of the human genome.

Visiting newly minted tech titans in the featureless industrial parks around Silicon Valley, we asked ourselves a central question: Can this simultaneous rise and demise—not only in California but across North America and the West, and even around the world—somehow be reconciled, bringing societies back into balance? Inevitably that question pointed to the political culture that had led California into its 2010 cul-de-sac.

In many ways the Golden State was giving us a preview of the populist eruption that would shake the United States in the 2016 presidential election. California's dysfunction traced to 1978, when voters passed Proposition 13, a landmark cap on property tax. That assertion of direct democracy—citizens making an end run around their own legislature and making law at the ballot box through the mechanism of the initiative—essentially shut off California's financial spigot. It set the stage for years of accumulating deficits by locking out revenues but locking in spending. Prop 13 was only the beginning of a revolt at the ballot box. In subsequent years, voters passed measures barring illegal immigrants from receiving public benefits and rejecting same-sex marriage. Both laws were later overturned by the courts.

Another ballot box rebellion had brought the bodybuilder and Hollywood superstar Arnold Schwarzenegger to power as governor in 2003. He was elected in an unprecedented recall that ousted Governor Gray Davis, a Democratic insider whom voters identified with the organized special interests of the establishment. Like

Trump in 2016, Schwarzenegger played to the frustrations of the average citizen: he didn't use Twitter, which hadn't been invented yet, but he did perform TV news–friendly stunts, such as dropping a car from a construction crane to dramatize his promise to cut vehicle fees, and brandishing a broom to symbolize sweeping the statehouse clean of special interests—all a tame version of populist antics.

To his credit, Schwarzenegger grew into the responsibility of office, and his legacy remains complex. He borrowed heavily, raising hefty deficits to compensate for taxes he and the state legislature cut, and he vetoed a proposal for a statewide health plan. But he also ultimately championed programs to help curb climate change and mitigate partisanship in primary elections.

Over the course of Schwarzenegger's two terms the contrasting fortunes of North America and Asia became more and more pronounced. Shortly after he left office, in 2012, his successor, Jerry Brown, hosted a visit by China's vice-president, the powerful soon-to-be-president Xi Jinping. When the discussion turned to finance, it was the American governor who did the asking: was there a way for China to help bankroll California's infrastructure, including a bullet train between San Francisco and Los Angeles that had been in the works for more than twenty years? The irony of the request was not lost on either leader. Brown, who had served a previous term as governor in the early 1980s, remembered having received a Chinese delegation led by Xi's father, then chief of Guangdong Province. Back then, it had been the Chinese seeking funds. The elder Xi had come in hopes of attracting investors to Guangdong's newly liberalized economic zone Shenzhen—now one of China's most prosperous cities, linked to the country's burgeoning 12,000-mile network of bullet train lines.

Looking for a way we could effectively help address the state's woes, we set up the Think Long Committee for California in October 2010. Its name was drawn from an injunction by former US secretary of state George Shultz, who became a member, to "think long" in order to make sound policy that endures the test of time. The nonpartisan group of thirteen also included former Speakers of the state assembly, a former state treasurer and governor, economists, labor union leaders and community advocates, high-tech entrepreneurs, and the just-retired chief justice of the California Supreme Court. Meeting once a month at Google headquarters in Mountain View for one year, it held hearings and issued the "Blueprint to Renew California" in 2011, following up with ballot and legislative measures to implement its recommendations. We discuss those recommendations in chapter 2.

At the time, the same kinds of concerns that came to the fore in California also arose globally as the world continued to reel after the 2009 financial crisis. To pursue our project at that level, we gathered a small group of former political leaders who had made real change—including former Brazilian president Fernando Henrique Cardoso, former German chancellor Gerhard Schroeder, and Felipe González—the former prime minister of Spain, for a discussion in the small bohemian apartment atop the Berggruen Museum in Berlin. Cardoso had brought wild inflation to heel with fiscal discipline in his enormous nation, drawing foreign investment back in and laying the groundwork for the "Brazilian Miracle" (which was later to unravel thanks to succeeding governments' populist policies). Schroeder turned a country that in the late 1990s was called "the sick man of Europe" into one of the most successful economies in the world by introducing more flexibility in the labor market and reforming welfare. González had nursed his country into its first years of democracy after the Franco dictatorship.

Huddled on two adjacent couches amid shelves stacked with art books about the works of Picasso, Giacometti, Matisse, and Klee exhibited in the galleries below, we candidly questioned whether a group of political has-beens could offer anything useful. Our honest answer was yes: out of office they could stand back and look at solutions to problems in a long-term, big-picture perspective, free from the daily demands of power and looming elections but knowing at the same time what it takes practically to make change happen. All agreed that such a group could be effective only if it engaged the rising powerhouse of China. So, from Berlin, we flew to Beijing to seek out a senior Chinese participant who no longer held an official position but remained influential. We were able to recruit one of the Middle Kingdom's more respected political elders, Zheng Bijian, author of China's "peaceful rise" and "community of convergent interests" doctrines and the longtime doyen of the Central Party School, the very heart of the system through which all top leaders must pass.

Based on those conversations, we established a group of statesmen and stateswomen, global intellectuals such as Nobel laureates Amartya Sen and Joseph Stiglitz, and tech leaders from Google, Twitter, LinkedIn, and, later, Snapchat and Alibaba to address issues that spanned both the major advanced and the emerging economies. The idea was to marry experience with rigorous thinking and, at the same time, to elicit challenges from innovators who came at problems from outside the box. In the initial years this group, the 21st Century Council, met with the chair of the G-20 to advise on the summit agenda. In later years we have met on a regular basis with President Xi Jinping and other senior leaders in Beijing to maintain a bridge of understanding with the world's preeminent rising power.

Back in California, our initial focus of concern, we saw cause for hope by the time of this writing. The return of competent, fiscally responsible, and experienced leadership when Jerry Brown was once again elected to the governorship in 2012 was a major factor in the turnaround. But citizen-driven reforms were also decisive, as they addressed many of the challenges that most concerned us in 2010. Chief among those were the redrawing of election districts by citizen commissions instead of the partisan legislature, undoing decades of damage from gerrymandering, and the introduction of a simple-majority vote on budgets (which broke the ongoing gridlock). The Think Long Committee for California and its allies helped tame direct democracy in the state by passing legislation that added transparency, deliberation, and negotiation with the legislature into the citizen's ballot-initiative process.

California is again showing the way to the future as a climate-friendly, diverse, "post-immigrant" state where, since 2000, most of the "majority-minority" residents are native-born, with Latinos and Asians making up the bulk of the population. The state has surpassed Great Britain to become the fifth-largest economy in the world.[2] Under Governor Brown's leadership, California took on the vanguard role of organizing a "network of the willing"— including Chinese president Xi—to pursue the fight against climate change in the wake of Washington's withdrawal from the Paris Climate Accord.

Yet even as California is beginning to master its challenges, the United States, like the rest of the Western democracies, has entered an era of peril. The disconnect between rise and demise remains as we identified it in Los Angeles back in 2010—only magnified to a broader, even worldwide level. Our experiences in California, combined with the lessons we've learned through our global network of relationships, have suggested to us ways we might renovate systems of governance that are failing their citizens by failing to adapt to fundamental changes under way in the first quarter of the twenty-first century.

The reader will note that throughout the book, as in this preface, we skip across scales, from local to national to global and back. This practice reflects not an inconsistency or confusion on our part but a recognition of the new reality of a dispersed distribution of power across systems that are integrated. The world today consists of a hodgepodge of jurisdictions, each trying out its own experiments in governance. Any relevant contribution to "taking back control" must take this into account. There is no longer any such thing as a local, national, or global strategy; they are all intermingled.

Los Angeles, California
June 2018

ACKNOWLEDGMENTS

First, we must thank Nathalia Ramos, who enthusiastically helped with the manuscript from the earliest days when this book was taking shape.

Our interactions with all the members of the Berggruen Institute's 21st Century Council over recent years have provided invaluable input. We are also especially thankful to all those who endured our interviews and discussions on rethinking globalization, from its economic to cultural and geopolitical dimensions. They include Dani Rodrik, Gordon Brown, Henry Kissinger, Raghuram Rajan, Laura Tyson, Larry Summers, Bill Clinton, Tony Blair, Kevin Rudd, Zhu Min, Shaukat Aziz, Elif Shafak, and Pankaj Mishra.

We were also greatly informed in our discussions on democracy and social media by Pierre Omidyar, Eric Schmidt, Toomas Ilves, Fernando Henrique Cardoso, and Canadian prime minister Justin Trudeau.

Our understanding of China has been deeply enhanced through our collaboration with Zheng Bijian and Feng Wei, who organized our two dialogues in Beijing with President Xi Jinping and others in the top leadership. Fu Ying, chair of the Foreign Affairs Committee of the National People's Congress, has enlightened us with her incisive views on the changing world order and China's role in it.

In many ways, our practical tutor in intelligent governance has been Governor Jerry Brown, who has put California back on the track of fiscal responsibility since the financial crash of 2008–9 while also leading a global "network of the willing" on climate change in the wake of the US withdrawal from the Paris Accord. In so many discussions over the years, we have learned statecraft from this master. It is hard to think of a rival to his experience and quality of judgment among leading political figures in the United States today.

Ron George, chief justice of the California Supreme Court from 1996 to 2010, graciously shared his constitutional brilliance and insights with us in formulating the initiative reform legislation that the Think Long Committee helped pass in 2014 and that Governor Brown signed into law. The indefatigable and ever-innovative Senator Bob Hertzberg shepherded that effort among a broad coalition of civic groups and through the legislature. He has also tirelessly moved the needle inch by inch to bring California's tax code into the twenty-first century. We are thankful to California's new governor, Gavin Newsom, for reading parts of this book and sharing his comments. Few have thought through so thoroughly the policy paths the Golden State needs to take in the years ahead.

Many of the key ideas in this book were first floated in one form or another in *The WorldPost,* the Berggruen Institute's publishing partnership with the *Washington Post.* The whole team— Executive Editor Kathleen Miles, Clarissa Pharr, Alex Gardels, Peter Mellgard, Rebecca Chao, and Rosa O'Hara—have availed us of the insights that *The WorldPost* has gathered from around the world.

Finally, but not at all least, of course, is the rest of the Berggruen Institute leadership team—Dawn Nakagawa and Nils Gilman, along with all their staff support, who have kept everything moving.

Rethinking Democracy, the Social Contract, and Globalization

The rise of populism in the West and the rise of China in the East have stirred a rethinking of how democratic systems work—or don't. The creation of new classes of winners and losers as a result of globalization and digital capitalism is also challenging how we think about the social contract and how wealth is shared.

The worst fear of America's Founders—that democracy would empower demagogues—was realized in the 2016 US presidential election, when the ballot box unleashed some of the darkest forces in the body politic. Similarly, in Europe an anti-establishment political awakening of both populism and right-wing neonationalism is consigning the mainstream centrist political parties that once dominated the post–World War II political order to the margins.

Donald Trump's election and the populist surge in Europe did not cause this crisis of governance. They are symptoms of the decay of democratic institutions across the West that, captured by the organized special interests of an insider establishment, have failed to address the dislocations of globalization and the disruptions of rapid technological change. To add danger to decay, the fevered partisans of populism are throwing out the baby with the bathwater, assaulting the very integrity of institutional checks and balances that guarantee the enduring survival of republics. The revolt against a moribund political class has transmuted into a revolt against governance itself.

Because neither the stakeholders of the waning status quo nor the upstarts of populism have offered any effective, systemic solutions to what ails the West, protracted polarization and paralysis have set in.

THE PARADOXES OF GOVERNANCE
IN THE DIGITAL AGE

These trials of the West are bound up with, and to a significant extent driven by, two related developments: the growing fragmentation of mass society into diverse tribes fortified by the participatory power of social media, and the advent of digital capitalism, which is divorcing productivity and wealth creation from employment and income.

We argue that these shifts present twin paradoxical challenges for governance.

First, the paradox of democracy in the age of peer-driven social networks is that, because there is more participation than ever before, never has the need been greater for countervailing practices and institutions to impartially establish facts, deliberate wise choices, mediate fair trade-offs, and forge consensus that can sustain long-term implementation of policies. Despite expectations that the Internet Age would create an informed public more capable of self-government than ever before in history, fake news, hate speech, and "alternative facts" have seriously degraded the civic discourse.

Second, the paradox of the political economy in the age of digital capitalism is that the more dynamic a perpetually innovating knowledge-driven economy is, the more robust a redefined safety net and opportunity web must be to cope with the steady disruption and gaps in wealth and power that will result.

To meet these challenges, we propose a novel approach to renovating democratic institutions that integrates new forms of direct participation into present practices of representative government while restoring to popular sovereignty the kind of deliberative ballast the American Founding Fathers thought so crucial to avoiding the suicide of republics. We further propose ways to spread wealth and opportunity fairly in a future in which intelligent machines are on track to displace labor, depress wages, and transform the nature of work to an unprecedented degree.

WHERE CHINA COMES IN

When populists rail against globalization that has undermined their standard of living through trade agreements, they mostly have China in mind. Few reflect that China was able to take maximum advantage of the post–Cold War US-led world order that promoted open trade and free markets precisely because of its consensus-driven and long-term-oriented one-party political system. China has shown the path to prosperity is not incompatible with authoritarian rule.

In this sense, China's tenacious rise over the past three decades holds up a harsh mirror to an increasingly dysfunctional West. The current US president, who rode an anti-globalization wave to power, relishes battling his way through every twenty-four-hour news cycle by firing off barbed tweets at sundry foes. By contrast, China's near-dictatorial leader has used his amassed clout to lay out a roadmap for the next thirty years.

If the price of political freedom is division and polarization, it comes at a steep opportunity cost. As the West—including Europe, riven now by populist and separatist movements—stalls in internal acrimony, China is boldly striding ahead. It has proactively set its sights on conquering the latest artificial intelligence technology, reviving the ancient Silk Road as "the next phase of globalization," taking the lead on climate change, and shaping the next world order in its image. If the West does not hear this wake-up call loud and clear, it is destined to somnambulate into second-class status on the world stage.

This is not, of course, to suggest in any way that the West turn toward autocracy and authoritarianism. Rather, it is to say that unless democracies look beyond the short-term horizon of the next election cycle and find ways to reach a governing consensus, they will be left in the dust by the oncoming future. If the discourse continues to deteriorate into a contest over who dominates the viral memes of the moment, and if democracy comes to mean sanctifying the splintering of society into a plethora of special interests, partisan tribes, and endless acronymic identities instead of seeking common ground, there is little hope of competing successfully with a unified juggernaut like China. Waiting for China to stumble is a foolish fallback.

Unlike the Soviet Union at the time of the *Sputnik* challenge in the late 1950s and early 1960s, China today possesses an economic and technological prowess the Soviet Union never remotely approached. Whether in conflict or cooperation, China will be a large presence in our future.

It is in that context that we examine the strengths and weakness of China's system as a spur to thinking through our own challenges. To turn the old Chinese saying toward ourselves, "The stones from hills yonder can polish jade at home."

TAKING BACK CONTROL

To set the frame for rethinking democracy and the political economy, we argue that the anxiety behind the populist reaction is rooted in the uncertainties posed by the great transformations under way, from the intrusions of globalization on how sovereign communities govern their affairs, to such rapid advances in technology as social media and robotics, to the increasingly multicultural composition of all societies. Change is so enormous that individuals and communities alike feel they are drowning in the swell of seemingly anonymous forces and want to "take back control" of their lives at a scale and stride they can manage. They crave the dignity of living in a society in which their identity matters and that attends to their concerns. Effectively aligning political practices and institutions so as to confront these challenges head-on will make the difference between a world falling apart and a world coming together.

Critics of globalization argue that nation-states and communities must retrieve the capacity to make decisions that reflect their way of life and maintain the integrity of their norms and institutions, decisions the maligned cosmopolitan caste has handed over to distant trade tribunals or other global institutions managed by strangers. Those decisions, they rightly say, ought to be made through "democratic deliberation" by sovereign peoples. Yet that neat logic ignores the reality of decay and dysfunction we have already noted. Therefore, "taking back control" must, first and foremost, mean renovating democratic practices and institutions themselves.

THE POLITICS OF RENOVATION

The most responsible course of change in modern societies is renovation. Rebellion is a cry for justice without a program for change. Populism, as we have seen, hurls pent-up passions at complex problems. Reform hews to the inertia of what has been. Revolution always ends in disaster because breaking from the past means purging the present in the name of the future.

Renovation is the point of equilibrium between creation and destruction, whereby what is valuable is saved and what is outmoded or dysfunctional is discarded. It entails a long march through society's institutions at a pace of change our incremental natures can absorb. Renovation shepherds the new into the old, buffering the damage of dislocation that at first outweighs longer-term benefits. In the new age of perpetual disruption, renovation is the constant of governance. Its aim is transition through evolutionary stability, within societies and in relations among nation-states and global networks.

In this book, we propose three ways to think about how to renovate democracy, the social contract, and global interconnectivity in order to take back control:

- Empowering participation without populism by integrating social networks and direct democracy into the system through the establishment of new mediating institutions that complement representative government
- Reconfiguring the social contract to protect workers instead of jobs while spreading the wealth of digital

capitalism by providing all citizens not only with the skills of the future but also with an equity share in "owning the robots"

· Harnessing globalization through "positive nationalism" at home, global cooperation where necessary, and partnership where interests converge to temper the strategic rivalry between China and the United States

These proposals, of course, do not exhaust the answers to the panoply of daunting challenges we have raised. But they do suggest ways we might think about how to change present social and political arrangements for addressing those challenges. We do not insist that we are somehow the font of all wisdom, but regard our endeavor as a point of departure that deepens and expands the debate. Without concrete propositions to criticize and amend, the discourse about change is only an airy exchange that fails to move the needle.

CHAPTER 1

Behind the Populist Surge

Donald Trump demonstrated in the 2016 US presidential election that a campaign of "alternative facts" and xenophobic invective against the world outside and perceived enemies within delivered over the latest direct-access technology—Twitter—can be the path to the top of the world's most powerful nation.

Fortunately, American civil society is among the most diverse and robust anywhere. And while it remains to be seen what Donald Trump's administration accomplishes (or is allowed to demolish), the alarm has sounded.

This situation has not emerged in a vacuum, but out of the decay of democracy itself in the past several decades. The lesson is clear for the United States and elsewhere: when an unresponsive elite forsakes average citizens in a system legitimated by popular sovereignty, demagogues who fashion themselves as tribunes of the people ride the rage to power. They inevitably end up wrecking what has been painstakingly built. Most damaging of all, and most difficult to repair, is the lost trust in the practices and institutions that enable sound government and constrain the use of power.

"Belief in the corruptibility of all institutions leads to a dead end of universal distrust," political scientist Francis Fukuyama warns. "American democracy, all democracy, will not survive a lack of belief in the possibility of impartial institutions; instead, partisan political combat will come to pervade every aspect of life."[1] And so it has. From a reading of history going back to ancient Rome, we know that this is the way republics unravel. That danger should be our uppermost concern today.

The populist wave, which spread from the 2016 Brexit and Trump elections to large constituencies across the Western democracies, has come at what is arguably one of the most promising times in human history. Prodigious leaps in technology, science, productive capacity, and global integration herald a future that humanity has only dreamt of in the past. Yet these ongoing great transformations seem to have triggered in their wake a great reaction among the multitude they have bypassed or threaten to uproot.

What is clear is that history is fast approaching an inflection point. We live either on the cusp of an entirely new era or on the brink of a return to an all-too-familiar, regressive, and darker past. How to reconcile these opposite trends is the daunting summons for governance in the decades ahead.

Governance is how communities invent and shape their destiny. It determines whether a society goes forward or backward. Like the homeostasis of all organisms, governance is the regulator, arbiter, and navigator of human affairs. It processes emotions through reason as the means by which societies not only survive but thrive by adapting to change.[2]

PERIL RESIDES WITHIN PROMISE

If we listen to our most visionary scientists and engineers, humanity is on the threshold of an age of health and abundance thanks to the convergence of such cutting-edge technologies as artificial intelligence, regenerative medicine, and the "internet of things." If we embrace the persistent dreams of economic thinkers, globalization that ties us all together promises to lift up everyone in a win-win scenario. Bill Gates, among others, has forecast that, thanks to innovations ranging from new vaccines to smart phones and mobile banking, "the lives of people in poor countries will improve faster in the next 15 years than at any other time in history."[3] Particularly in the advanced nations, the automation of labor opens a path to the end of drudgery and a world where scarcity no longer defines the human condition. Technologies that exploit renewable energy sources herald a new era of low-carbon growth that can cool the fever of global warming.

Yet, without appropriate governance, a young person from any of the impoverished regions to which Gates refers will likely use that smartphone to navigate a hazardous path northward as a refugee. And the robots that so greatly boost productivity could just as well generate wealth only for the few and displace jobs that pay a living wage, creating even deeper social inequality. Absent the restraining hand of governance, climate change will disrupt life as we know it on earth.

Signs of splintering are all around us not only in polarized partisanship but also in revived nativism and nationalism, ardent religious wars, and the reappearance of geopolitical blocs. In 2014 Pope Francis even declared that we are living through a "piecemeal Third World War."[4] Applied historians these days keep raising the analogy to 1914, when world war suddenly broke out after the "long peace" of the first globalization, during which nations were nearly as integrated through trade and investment as they are now. The historian and strategic thinker Walter Russell Mead has gone so far as to ask whether today "we are in a post-war or pre-war period."[5]

And none of us can say for sure at this moment whether the likes of Malala or Islamofascists, democracy or autocracy, will define the path ahead.

To reach breakthrough before breakdown involves, first of all, grasping the dynamics of the underlying turmoil. The truth is not only that both realities exist simultaneously but that one is a condition of the other. The fearful and fearsome reaction against growing inequality, social dislocation, and loss of identity in the midst of vast wealth creation, unprecedented mobility, and ubiquitous connectivity is a mutiny, really, against globalization so audacious and against technological change so rapid that it can barely be absorbed by our incremental nature. Change takes place at a digital pace our analog capacities can't process. In this accelerated era, future shock can feel like repeated blows in the living present to individuals, families, and communities alike. In this one world, it sometimes seems, a race is on between the newly empowered and the recently dispossessed.

This emergent world appears to us as a wholly unfamiliar rupture from patterns of the past that could frame a reassuring narrative going forward. Philosophers describe the new territory of the future as "plastic" or "liquid," shapelessly shifting as each disruptive innovation or abandoned certitude washes away whatever fleeting sense of meaning was only just embraced. A kind of foreboding of the times that have not yet arrived, a wariness about what's next, settles in. Novelists such as Jonathan

Franzen see a "perpetual anxiety" gripping society.[6] Similarly, Turkish novelist Orhan Pamuk, citing Wordsworth, speaks of "a strangeness in my mind," the sense that "I am not of this hour nor of this place."[7]

DISRUPTION, INSECURITY, AND IDENTITY

Philosophers and social thinkers have long noted the relationship between such anxiety or sense of threat and the reactive fortification of identity. The greater the threat—of violence, upheaval, or insecurity—the more rigid and "solitarist" identities become, as Amartya Sen noted in his seminal book *Identity and Violence*.[8] Intense threats, or the perception of them, demote plural influences in the lives of persons and communities alike and elevate a singular dimension to existential importance. At the personal level this shift is experienced as a deficit of dignity. Conversely, stability, security, and inclusivity generate adaptive identities with plural dimensions.

We've seen this fearful impulse before. In the late nineteenth and early twentieth centuries, widespread optimism, manifested so magnificently by London's Crystal Palace in 1851 and numerous subsequent world fairs and expositions, resulted from the great leaps in industrialization, urbanization, energy, communications, and transportation, as well as the transformation of the household with labor-saving appliances. But the surface sheen masked deep anxiety and resentment as settled patterns of life across the old empires of Europe were turned upside-down and uprooted. Elites and masses alike sought refuge in nationalism, racial solidarity, or class allegiance. Then, suddenly in the summer of 1914, it all burst to the fore in World War I, which ended with 16 million senseless deaths, only to lay the groundwork for the next calamity less than two decades later, which culminated in a shattered European continent, Auschwitz, the rape of Nanjing, and the nuclear devastation of Japanese cities.

LUTHER'S 95 THESES AND TWITTER'S 280 CHARACTERS

In history, breakdown has inevitably followed transformational technological breakthroughs and openings to other cultures, unless political institutions have adapted to the resulting power shift. Religious wars in the West, we recall, erupted in the wake of the invention of the Gutenberg press, which enabled the Christian scriptures to appear in vernacular languages, thus diminishing the authority of the Church in faraway Rome and empowering individuals and sects—the so-called Protestant "priesthood of all believers"—to interpret the scriptures by their own lights. Today's 280 Twitter characters, posted in cyberspace by anyone and everyone, are no less disruptive than Martin Luther's 95 Theses nailed to the Wittenberg Castle church door in 1517. In his study of hierarchies and networks, *The Square and the Tower,* historian Niall Ferguson credits the Reformation with not only laying the ground for the Scientific Revolution and the Enlightenment but also instigating the religious wars that spanned more than a century from 1524 to 1648. "The printing press," which facilitated the Reformation's spread, he writes, "has justly been called 'a decisive point of no return in human history.'"[9]

Similarly, the spread of urbanization and industrialization during the eighteenth and nineteenth centuries disrupted the feudal hierarchies and traditional ways of life of predominantly rural societies, leading to the breakup of empires and, ultimately, world war. Today, the maturation of a globally integrated world replete with cross-cultural flows of people, goods, capital, and information, not to mention the perpetual disruptions of digital capitalism, all pose tough new challenges. Technology always speeds ahead of politics, but today it both closes some gaps and widens others at a swifter clip. The rapid opening of societies to one another through telecom-, high-tech-, and logistics-enabled global economic integration has brought a once-impoverished China of peasant villages face-to-face as an equal with the American superpower in the mere forty years since the end of Maoism, challenging the pride of place of the resentful old order.

The lesson here is that political and cultural logic, rooted in emotion, identity, and ways of life cultivated among one's own kind, operates in a wholly different dimension than the rational and universalizing ethos of economics and technology. Far from moving forward in lock-step progress, when they meet, they clash.

Regrettably, historical experience has demonstrated over and over again that, when real or perceived threats abound, practical politics departs from rational discourse and centers on friends versus enemies; us versus them.[10] It focuses on organizing the survival and sustenance of a community as defined by those who are not part of it. Politics, not least in the present wave of populism across the Western democracies, is rooted in the particular soil of place and not in the universal territory of humanity as a whole or the "common good." Donald Trump, British prime minister Theresa May, and other leaders of the revolt against the cosmopolitan caste could not be clearer. "There is no such thing as a global anthem, a global currency, or a global flag," Trump has said.[11]

Similarly, May has proclaimed, "If you believe you are a citizen of the world, you are a citizen of nowhere. You don't know what citizenship means."[12] In his book *The Road to Somewhere: The Populist Revolt and the Future of Politics*, David Goodhart puts his finger on the divide between the "anywheres" of a rootless, mobile elite and the "somewheres" rooted in community.[13] In the real world, however much elites may feel global, most people react local.

WHAT ABOUT US?

In the fall of 2016, Sigmar Gabriel, then Germany's vice-chancellor, concisely captured the backlash roiling politics in his country and the rest of Europe. "As the average citizens see it," he said, "first the authorities spent billions on bailing out the banks, and now are spending generously on refugees from war-torn Syria and elsewhere—meanwhile cutting back on pensions, unemployment payments and other social benefits through austerity policies. 'What about us?' they ask." When people retreat into their own suffering, better angels lose their wings. That attitude may not make saints of citizens, but neither does it make them sinners.

In the 2016 US presidential race, Donald Trump tapped into this kind of disaffection. His mantra that the cosmopolitan caste had opened the doors wide to immigrants and the globalizing theft of manufacturing while failing to first provide security, protect jobs, and promote the interests of ordinary citizens was convincing enough to win the day. And he is not entirely wrong.

In short, what animates today's nationalist sentiments, and paradoxically ties them together across borders, is a double antipathy. The disparate nationalist forces are revolting against both the faceless forces of global integration represented by huge multinational companies, trade agreements, or Brussels "Eurocrats,"[14] and the immediate face-to-face presence of immigrants and refugees whom they see as despoiling their own national identities.

What is clear is that both real and imagined issues have become conflated in the mounting backlash against global integration. These concerns merge into a generalized anxiety, fed by social media's mix of truths and untruths, an anxiety that expresses itself in the distrust of public institutions and governing elites.

Even in cases where politics has moved away from populism—most notably the election of the nonpartisan, post-ideological Emmanuel Macron in France in 2017—the society underneath still roils. In that election, Marine Le Pen, who sought to inflame anxieties over immigration and national identity, garnered a substantial 34 percent of the vote. More than one-third of the electorate abstained or cast null ballots, and more than 50 percent of the youth vote went to Le Pen or to the candidate on the other side of the spectrum, the far-left Jean-Luc Melanchon.[15] In the German elections in 2017, Angela Merkel's centrist party attained only 33 percent of the vote—the same percentage as Le Pen in France—while a neonationalist party garnered enough votes to enter the Bundestag for the first time since the Nazis.

If any further proof were needed of the unsettled body politic in Europe, Italy's elections in March 2018 provide it. The wildly anti-establishment Five Star Movement won the largest share of votes—over 33 percent—while the mainstream parties met their biggest loss since World War II.

In an era of profound cultural transformation, elections and referendums settle little. For those who are nostalgic for an ideal past, the challenges of a complex future wrought by globalization, digital disruption, and increasing cultural diversity remain a threat. For those looking ahead, going back solves nothing. The present political stalemate, which seems to divide nearly every society in half, is only the first act, not the last. It is the beginning, not the end, of the story of societies in fluid transition.

GOD AND COMPUTERS

Politics thus simply reflects the deeper dilemmas of societies in transition. The triumph of modernity in recent centuries— of the universal and rational Enlightenment worldview that spawned globalization and technological advance—has meant not the eradication of deep culture or religious and tribal impulses but rather their displacement. As the French philosopher Regis Debray writes, "The anachronistic and the archaic all have their place in modern politics because 'modern' does not designate a location in time but a position in the terracing of influences, or determinations: not the outmoded but the substratum; not the antiquated but the profound; not the outdated but the repressed."[16] It was this clear-minded perspective on human nature that prompted Debray to predict way back in 1986, long before the Islamic State or Facebook, that the twenty-first century would feature both "God and computers."[17] Deep culture always returns to shape a society in a way similar to how a person's emotional subconscious is always biting at the heels of rational cognition. Culture is the substructure and economics and politics are the superstructure, not vice versa as modern thought would have it. With this insight, Debray also foresaw the nationalist backlash that has now consumed the once-globalizing West by arguing that if borders don't secure cultural affinity, walls will be erected in their place as an affirmation of threatened identity. "Borders," he has written, "are a vaccine against the epidemic of walls."[18]

While it is true that culture is conservative, it is never static and is always evolving into new hybrid forms through contact with others. But its fusions and frictions rarely balance out, and when they do, it is only over very long periods of time. What appears to be cross-pollination can end up as mere "borrowed surfaces," while the deeper *Volksgeist,* the values and ways of life historically embedded in a nation or a tribe, remains as the foundation of identity.

Modernity maintains a superstitious faith in change. But change is no more an unalloyed good than a romanticized traditional order. All we know is that the pursuit of pure states of being—whether of ideal pasts, utopian futures, superior races, or true religions—is in the end totalitarian and in conflict with the diverse disposition of human nature.

The superficiality of commerce and technology no doubt also accounts for Westerners' surprise when cultures such as neo-Confucian China or neo-Ottoman Turkey do not evolve according to the expectation that they will "become like us" but instead chart a future rooted in their own past. Liberal modernizers from the West are only now catching on to the fact that rising prosperity in China has not dented the civilizational weight of centralized institutions and authoritarian, if pragmatic, rule stretching back millennia. They are also coming to terms now with the fact that democratic modernization from below in Turkey has taken that country further away from secularism and closer to its Ottoman past, ruling sultan and all.

Thus, while universal reason and efficiency engender the convergence we see today with globalization and the spread of technology, the cultural and political imagination engender the opposite when threatened—a divergent search for shelter within the familiar ways of life that register a dignity of recognition among one's own kind and constitute identity against the swell of anonymous forces.

In the end, it is this *perceived loss of control over one's destiny*—whether as a result of technological change, globalization, immigration, or some combination of these—that is at the root of the backlash. Identity politics is an effort to create a safe and familiar space for you and your kind in a world of tumult fomented by strangers. The politics of renovation for which we argue avoids this binary error through cherishing core values while adapting pragmatically to what works in new circumstances that arise.

The foremost challenge today is how to reestablish—on new terms—this sense of control that has been lost, thus avoiding social upheaval so disruptive that the bold leaps forward of recent decades will propel our societies several reactionary steps backward into the kind of wars and divisions we saw in the twentieth century, or, worse, on terms that propel us into some postmodern version of the Dark Ages of medieval Europe.

If there is any chance of heading off breakdown, governance must adapt to new realities by embracing the rising participatory power of social networks while seizing the opportunities and addressing the insecurities generated by globalization and the knowledge-driven innovation economy.

Reestablishing a common sense of belonging and ownership of the future is the precondition for communities "taking back control." That means, above all, renovating the practices and institutions of democratic deliberation. Although tackling this objective does not answer all the anxieties and insecurities that are churning our societies, it precedes all other issues in importance since it is the platform through which open societies make the key choices about their future. Unless the dysfunction is repaired, there is little hope of reaching a governing consensus that responds to challenges on both the near and the far horizon.

CHAPTER 2

Renovating Democracy

In the West, the contest over contrasting visions of the future must be settled through the practices and institutions of democratic deliberation. If those institutional arrangements have decayed or become outmoded due to changes in society and technology, renovating them under the new conditions is the most pressing challenge from which all else follows. Simply returning "our" partisans to the halls of power only reproduces the problem. Neither a turn toward autocracy nor lame attachment to forms of democratic government that have become dysfunctional offers an answer to the question of how to govern open societies in the twenty-first century.

REPRESENTATIVE GOVERNMENT IN CRISIS

Fernando Henrique Cardoso—or FHC, as he is colloquially known, is a rare bird among political species from a nation associated most with its Amazon rainforest. Intellectuals in power are not much in evidence these days. A world-renowned sociologist, Cardoso was elected president of Brazil for two terms between 1995 and 2003. As a scholar he is best known for his *dependencia* theory. It postulates that so-called countries of the periphery are impoverished by the outflow of resources to rich "core nations"; peripheral countries can never escape underdevelopment without both savings of their own and investment and the transfer of technology from abroad. As president, Cardoso put theory into practice, privatizing some state industries to attract investment and taming hyperinflation by imposing fiscal discipline. He thus laid the groundwork for what would later be called the Brazilian miracle, which introduced both rapid growth and diminishing inequality—before it all ran into trouble in later years through a combination of corruption and populist indifference to fiscal responsibility.

So when the avuncular FHC speaks about what ails Brazil today, along with the advanced Western nations, he is worth listening to. In the wake of months of mass demonstrations and the impeachment of Brazilian president Dilma Roussef in 2016, Cardoso brought both the instincts of a veteran politico and the keen observations of a social scientist to the analysis of the common challenges to democracy everywhere it is established. His insights are worth quoting at length:

> We are indeed witnessing in Brazil—as in the traditional democracies of the West—the impact of great economic and technological transformations. National states are weakened by globalization[;] societies are increasingly structurally fragmented by a new division of labor and exposed to the tensions and imbalances of growing cultural diversity. All this leads to anxiety and fear about the future, with uncertainty over how to preserve social cohesion, ensure jobs, and reduce inequality.

In democracies in crisis, the class differences mix up with other forms of social identity. Established political parties are bound to lose space. Narratives that seek to connect with and address the grievances of disempowered masses fill the void left by the demise of representative democracy.

This is a situation fraught with risk. In the regions where it is more deeply rooted—the Americas and Europe—representative democracy is in crisis. At the core of this crisis is the widening gap between people's aspirations and the capacity of political institutions to respond to the demands of society. It is one of the ironies of our age that this deficit of trust in political institutions coexists with the rise of citizens capable of making the choices that shape their lives and influence the future of their societies.

To put it in a nutshell, our challenge is to bridge the gap between demos and res publica, between people and the institutions of public interest, reweaving the threads that may reconnect the political system with the demands of society.[1]

Indeed, the risk of which the respected former president warns was realized in October 2018, when the far-right "Trump of the tropics," Jair Bolsonaro, won the presidential election. Cardoso is quite right to claim that the social cohesion that once enabled political consensus has eroded. Indeed, a new segregation is emerging as a combined result of *the demise of socializing institutions and the rise of polarizing norms and practices.* Mandatory universal military or civic service is gone in most liberal societies. Universal public education in which all classes, races, and ethnicities mingle has been left to less-well-off communities while the top 20 percent head off to private education from pre-school to university. Add to this the inequality that is growing with the widening bifurcation of the digital economy into high- and low-wage sectors, which translates into neighborhood segregation through real estate pricing.

At the same time, the mainstream media play to cultural niches in highly competitive markets, while the business model of social media companies maximizes virality among the like-minded. This division of the social imagination into silos in which stereotypes replace real experience with others both fuels and is amplified in the discourse of demagogic politics.

These symbiotic forces contribute mightily to the disconnect Cardoso identifies between society and the politics of consensus.

Cardoso's summation of today's crisis of governance closely tracks the views of another South American intellectual, Moises Naim. Once Venezuela's minister of trade and industry and executive director of the World Bank, Naim later served as editor of *Foreign Policy* magazine. In his book *The End of Power*, Naim argues that power has become so diffused that the old ways of top-down governance—whether in states, corporations, or the Catholic Church—are no longer effective. "Power is spreading," he writes, "and long-established big powers are increasingly being challenged by newer and smaller ones. And those who have more power are constrained in the ways they can use it . . . power is easy to get, harder to use, and easier to lose."[2] As a result, Naim expects "a revolutionary wave of political and institutional innovations" unseen since the end of World War II. Like Cardoso, he sees the central political goal of our time as "restoring trust, reinventing political parties, finding new ways in which average citizens can meaningfully participate in the political process, creating new mechanisms of effective governance, limiting the worst aspects of checks and balances while averting excesses in the concentration of accountable power."[3] The challenge in every country lies in designing new practices and institutions that harness the dynamic forces of globalization from above as well as the micropower constituencies from below to meet awakened demands for meaningful participation.

Francis Fukuyama assesses the challenge to US democracy from a related angle. He observes that "the efficiency of consensual decision-making deteriorates rapidly as groups become more diverse and as their size increases." As the cogency of the two major US political parties has weakened, organized special interests, from evangelical Christians to environmental fundamentalists, teachers' unions, big tech, and the financial and gun lobbies, have strengthened their clout. These trends have transformed American democracy into a "vetocracy," in which such interests block any changes that would diminish the spoils derived from the status quo that favors them. According to Fukuyama, "in terms of the sheer number of veto players, the American political system is an outlier among contemporary democracies. It has become unbalanced and in certain areas has acquired too many checks and balances which raise the cost of collective action, sometimes making it impossible altogether." Gridlock has taken hold as the extreme ideological edges have increased their influence within the weakened mainstream parties. "When polarization confronts America's Madisonian check-and-balance political system, the result is particularly devastating."[4] The result, Fukuyama concludes, is that the "decayed" American political system is "less and less able to represent majority interests but gives excessive representation to the views of interest groups and activist organizations that collectively do not add up to a sovereign American people."

Anti-elite populism has been the broad response to this disconnect between a captured governing class and those who see the system as not working for them. "Populism appeals to the 'will of people,'" says philosopher Julian Baggini, "but is actually profoundly undemocratic. Democracy is about the negotiation of competing interests, the balancing of different values. Populism, in contrast, is a kind of mob rule. Where there is complexity, it offers simple solutions. Instead of seeking common ground, it looks to exaggerate the differences between them and us. The unquestioned righteousness of its own cause and means to its ends leads to the demonization of those it opposes."[5] One could not find a better description of present-day politics in the United States and Great Britain, as well as some areas of Continental Europe. In such an environment of extreme polarization, consensual truths and moderation are seen as a betrayal.

THE PARTICIPATORY POWER OF SOCIAL MEDIA

In our view, the disaffection with and distrust in governing institutions that all the above-quoted thinkers observe has gained more traction than ever before because of the participatory power of social media. It levels the playing field of information among amateurs, professionals, and meritocratic experts. As a platform open to all, social media challenge the custodianship of elites and even the legitimacy of representative democracy. This platform heralds a new distribution of power that goes hand in hand with Western publics' increasing preference for the direct democracy of referenda and citizens' initiatives. We've seen the highly disruptive Catalan independence and Brexit votes. Populist movements and insurgent parties elsewhere across Europe, such as the Five Star Movement in Italy, are all proposing referendum-driven and plebiscitary democracy as the way to cope with pressing issues, including European integration and immigration.[6] In Mexico, President Andrés Manuel López Obrado has promised to "let the people decide" on the big controversial issues through "participatory democracy." "The idea that somehow any decision reached any-time by majority rule is necessarily 'democratic' is a perversion of the term," economist Kenneth Rogoff wrote after Great Britain's vote to leave the European Union. "This isn't democracy; it is Russian roulette for republics."[7] We couldn't agree more.

Yet a new sensibility has been unleashed: if ordinary citizens believe they can know as much as those who would govern them, and who are governing them badly, who needs governing institutions? Why can't the disgruntled public, connected by social media, just make decisions on its own? Such an idea fits easily with the notion that, since the Information Age has created a citizenry more informed than at any time in history, intermediaries, such as representatives in an assembly or policy experts, can be dispensed with.

This line of thinking was perhaps best expressed by Mark Zuckerberg in an open letter announcing Facebook's initial public offering in 2012: "By giving people the power to share, we are starting to see people make their voices heard on a different scale from what has historically been possible. These voices will increase in number and volume. They cannot be ignored. Over time, we expect governments will become more responsive to issues and concerns raised directly by all their people rather than through intermediaries controlled by a select few."[8] Zuckerberg certainly had his finger on the pulse of his time. Political awakenings were erupting everywhere across the globe. People fed up in one way or another with unresponsive elites had begun demanding the dignity of meaningful participation in setting the rules that govern their lives. Through social media they now had the wherewithal to share and organize their ill temper or utopian hopes.

This prospect has proved true, however, not only for the forces of inclusion, such as we saw in the Arab Spring—those that Zuckerberg clearly had in mind. The tools of social media and direct democracy are also available to the forces of exclusion, as we saw most clearly in the Brexit and Trump campaigns—as well as in the Russian efforts to sow racial animosity and anti–Hillary Clinton sentiment by manipulating social media during the 2016 election.

As direct democracy increasingly becomes the governing practice of choice by proliferating constituencies whose voice is amplified by social media, the countervailing institutions of deliberation must be equally strengthened. The raw, unprocessed expression of discontent with governing elites alone leads to the "dumb mob"—both on social media and at the ballot box. Only mediated feedback formulated as responsive policies can lead to a collectively intelligent response.

Ask Wael Ghonim. He knows. "I once said, 'If you want to liberate a society, all you need is the Internet.' I was wrong. I said those words back in 2011, when a Facebook page I anonymously created helped spark the Egyptian revolution. The Arab Spring revealed social media's greatest potential, but it also exposed its greatest shortcomings. The same tool that united us to topple dictators eventually tore us apart" through echo-chamber polarization, misinformation, and toxic hate speech.[9] During the heady days of the Arab Spring in Cairo, Ghonim came to recognize that Facebook's "mobocracy algorithm," which is designed to monetize attention by pushing together those who share the same passions and prejudices, has a deleterious, instead of liberating, impact.[10]

In short, the same medium that so effectively transmits a howling message of change also undermines the ability to make it. Social media amplify the human tendency to bind with one's own kind. They reduce complex social challenges to mobilizing slogans that reverberate in echo chambers of the like-minded, rather than providing a platform for persuasion, dialogue, and the negotiation necessary for consensus. They serially divide the body politic among itself. Polarization rigidifies. Paralysis and gridlock set in. Alternatives in the form of an authoritarian and demagogic strongman start to look attractive as the way to bring order out of chaos.

Speaking Truth to Social Media

These days, Ghonim has turned his attention to filtering social media. He proposes a "meritocratic algorithm" to sort out junk and quality, untruth and truth, as the basis of a new business model beyond silos and "likes." Where once social media were hailed as a new means of speaking truth to power, now, he believes, the challenge is to speak truth to social media.[11]

Ghonim's concern closely parallels that of political scientist Philip Pettit, who has long argued that republican government relies on an encompassing array of institutions and practices that take all interests into account, not simply "empowering the collective will" of the majority or plurality that happens to turn up for a given poll. This applies as well to today's peer-driven media that have become the modern public square. For Petit what is required is a "depoliticized" space in which to deliberate choices, sort out truth from falsehood, and make trade-offs among contending priorities. In Pettit's view, there is "no democratization without depoliticization" through the interposition of impartial mediating bodies.[12]

A Berggruen Institute working group that included participants from Facebook and Google as well as Ghonim and others met in Silicon Valley in 2017 to address the risks that social media and the deteriorating health of our information ecosystem pose to democracy. The group concluded that large social network platforms must indeed be considered "media" outlets with editorial responsibilities. Algorithms are, after all, editorial decisions. Their design determines what is published and promoted and what is not. As such, algorithms must be subject to rules of transparency and accountability.

The main conflict in sorting out this issue is the existential threat to democratic governance from self-referential silos of fake news, alternative facts, and hate speech that are at odds with the bottom-line business model of social media platforms based on monetizing attention through engagement and virality, whatever the truth content of information. In this regard, philosopher Onora O'Neill is right to criticize what she calls "cyber romantics," who defend absolute free speech as the be all and end all. The truth content and verified trustworthiness of information and sources, she contends, is equally important in "the ethics of communication."[13]

In European countries and China, governments have few qualms about stepping in and making the rules. China has deployed hundreds of thousands of censors to track social media and delete troubling posts. Through its Network Enforcement Act, Germany imposes a stiff fine of 50 million euros for hate speech or fake news if not removed from the Web. "The big internet platforms, through their algorithms, have become an eye of the needle which diverse media must pass through [to access their users]," German chancellor Angela Merkel warned when she called on Facebook and others to make their algorithms transparent so users know how they are being steered.[14] This whole approach deeply troubles critics who point out that, if unregulated, it subcontracts decisions over free speech in Germany to America's high-tech companies. These critics believe that the German courts, not Mark Zuckerberg, should be making such decisions.[15] On the other hand, some worry that there is the danger of regulators going too far. As the EU digital commissioner put it: "Fake news is bad, but a ministry of truth is worse."[16]

In the United States, where the First Amendment guarantee of free speech is considered absolute, the answer has so far involved civil society groups pressuring the information industry to self-regulate by establishing industry-wide standards and a common code of conduct. One such code under discussion would, for example, focus on suppressing distribution of information—the megaphone effect—rather than suppressing the information itself. It would also ban the use of bots—inauthentic amplifiers—so that artificial intelligence, in effect, does not become a participant in politics. This approach tracks the "unsafe at any speed" auto safety regulations of the 1970s, which, rather than prohibit driving, required seat belts for all passengers.[17] In California, legislation has been proposed to require social media companies to identify online interventions made by bots.[18]

Companies should be encouraged, as Ghonim has suggested, to design algorithms that promote quality information instead of junk, that "reward reality" over fake news and alternative facts. More radical ideas include employing the distributed technology of blockchain, whereby data are securely stored across networks instead of with monopolistic platforms. This would redecentralize the internet so that big-tech companies can no longer channel connectivity through their proprietary algorithms and exploit personal data for their own profit.

As is already happening to some extent, independent, "third party" monitors have been engaged to check facts and search for hate speech. These should be established as permanent watchdogs. Some have suggested that "societal impact reviews," not unlike environmental impact reports, ought to be required for new development projects. A further step seems eminently sensible: the large social network platforms should go beyond outsourcing to "third parties" and set up a stream of revenue to fund the "Fourth Estate"—the sort of full-fledged, quality journalism that their business model is driving out of existence

Indeed, in the wake of the 2016 election even Mark Zuckerberg was forced to think again. He wrote in a lengthy communiqué to Facebook shareholders in February 2017: "Social media is a short-form medium where resonant messages get amplified many times. This rewards simplicity and discourages nuance. At its best, this focuses messages and exposes people to different ideas. At its worst, it oversimplifies important topics and pushes us towards extremes." News and information sensationalized to maximize views, Zuckerberg continued, is now his top concern. "Sensationalism moves people away from balanced nuanced opinions towards polarized extremes. If this continues and we lose common understanding, then even if we eliminated all misinformation, people would just emphasize different sets of facts to fit their polarized opinions. That's why I'm so worried about sensationalism in media."[19]

That is the crisis now. It involves not just Facebook but all social media platforms. Yet media these days evolve rapidly. One hope, as Eric Schmidt of Alphabet, Google's parent company, has expressed it, is that the "mobocratic algorithm" and echo-chambers of the like-minded are only early responses to an overwhelming deluge of information that is new to human experience. In time, perhaps in proportion to the ever-greater cascade of data, curation will again emerge as a key to avoiding overload.[20] The formidable challenge will lie in reestablishing curatorial authority, like political authority? On what basis? By what criteria?

Pierre Omidyar, a cofounder of eBay and the chair of the Berggruen Institute's social media working group, offers some suggestions. He argues that, outside mathematics, there is no one objective truth, only consensual truth agreed upon by knowledgeable people—"experts"—who are transparent about the methods by which they gather their data and arrive at their conclusions. With media, transparency implies conveying to readers and viewers how information and sources are verified and why they are credible. Even when the media meet this obligation, it is human nature for individuals to process information through their own biases. For Omidyar, the best way to overcome people's biases is not just to challenge one view with another, but to expose the contradictions in an argument that confirm or raise doubts about its value as truth. Exposure to multiple, instead of merely opposing, arguments, Omidyar argues, would create a critical space for comparing and contrasting different points of view.[21]

Like political revolutions, technological revolutions tend to unfold in phases. First comes the liberating breakthrough from the old order, burnished with utopian ideals. Next comes the reaction to abuses that inevitably arise from embarking on a new path for which there are no rules, especially for the first movers, who become the new masters. Finally, a new governing order is established that sorts out the mistakes and excesses from the benefits of transformational change and eliminates or tempers the former. This, it seems—let's hope—is where we are today.

The ultimate consequence if we fail to control social media is the universalization of nihilism, a condition in which the whole notion of consensual truth would collapse and the subjectivization of fact would fill the vacuum—the sad remains of the heyday of Enlightenment values. Aviv Ovadya, chief technologist at the University of Michigan's Center for Social Media Responsibility, sees on the horizon a "catastrophic failure of the marketplace of ideas," where "no one believes anything or everyone believes lies." He calls it the "infopocalypse."[22]

These penetrating observations notwithstanding, the only tool secular democracies have for establishing consensual truths that inform a governing narrative is reasoned deliberation. But that tool itself has to be reconfigured by absorbing and transforming the very forces that are undermining it.

The democratization of information through digital media is a close cousin of direct democracy in governance. Both media and governance need disinterested and impartial institutions. In the case of governance, such institutions permit contending, often unequal, interests to negotiate trade-offs. In the media, they sort out truth claims among the unlike-minded and create platforms that enable dialogue across tribal boundaries. As the philosopher of consciousness Daniel Dennett observes, without institutions or practices that can establish and preserve credibility, there is no solid ground for democratic discourse. Instead, what we will see—and in fact are already seeing—is "an arms race of ploy and counterploy" in which the whole notion of objectivity is a casualty of that battle of truths.[23]

Based on the foregoing analysis, we now take the next step that few books of this nature do: we propose a redesign of our democratic institutions that responds both to the oldest challenges of governance and to the newest developments in the evolution of society and technology.

The Paradox of Governance in the Digital Age

The paradox of governance in the age of social networks is that, precisely because there is more participation than ever before in peer-driven media and because these contributions are unchecked by factual observation, never has the need been greater for countervailing practices and institutions to establish facts, deliberate wise choices, mediate fair trade-offs, and forge consensus that can sustain long-term implementation of policies.

If contemporary democracies are to compete successfully with autocratic systems on the world stage while avoiding their own suicide through polarization and paralysis fueled by untrustworthy information, they need radical renovation that responds to the forces undermining them. Above all, such a renovation must engage the participatory power of social media and the increasing preference of publics for direct democracy by designing new, impartial institutions and practices that interpose a deliberative check against the false claims, misinformation, intolerance, and magical thinking that come along with the immediate wash of networked popular sentiment.

Such a renovation that embraces participation without devolving into populism would draw on the wisdom of the Founders, who believed that institutions of delegated authority are necessary to "enlarge the public view."[24] It would draw as well from the innovations made by US states during the Progressive movement at the turn of the twentieth century. The Progressives sought to combine the direct democracy of the ballot initiative—which they introduced so that citizens could make laws directly—with smart government administered by nonpartisan professionals and experts.

Accordingly, a key innovation for democracy today would be to proactively solicit priority concerns from the public through open platforms, empower knowledgeable officials to process those concerns into effective and consensual policy responses on an impartial basis, and then go back to citizens directly for approval of those proposals at the ballot box before they become law.

Studies show that most citizens are less partisan and more open to pragmatic solutions than are the parties vying for power.[25] Such a revision in the way self-government works would complement representative democracy and at the same time compensate for its waning legitimacy in our age of distributed power. It would provide a robust avenue for citizens to initiate action outside legislatures that are most often locked up by the established parties and organized special interests that have the time and money to win elections and maintain a lobby-hold on those they elect.

As faith in representative government falters, public opinion polls show support for such a fresh approach. According to a global poll conducted by the Pew Research Center in October 2017, 66 percent of respondents preferred a system in which "citizens, not elected officials, vote directly on major issues to decide what becomes law." At the same time, 49 percent would approve of a system in which "experts, not elected officials, make key decisions."[26]

To consider such an alternative requires rethinking whether representative democracy in which large and cogent political parties compete for power still suits today's realities as the main institutional arrangement for obtaining consent of the governed.

Post-party Politics?

For some, the crisis of representative democracy suggests the need to forge strong new parties that can bring the new and disparate constituencies of today's highly diverse societies under one big tent, thus enabling a governing consensus by whichever party or parties dominate elections. Plenty of evidence suggests, however, that the Industrial Age model of cohesive, mass political parties with which the public loyally identifies has been disrupted, perhaps fatally. They seem to be splintering beyond repair, going the way of lifetime employment and the mainstream media. Just as we now have just-in-time manufacturing, we may be headed toward just-in-time politics. A post-party politics may be emerging in which coalitions of the willing mobilize around specific issues, seek effective remedy, and disband, and new coalitions are formed in order to move on to the next issue. Just as fragmentation and flexibility have entered the labor market as a permanent feature, they have entered the political marketplace as well.

In a discussion with one of the authors in Lisbon in March 2107, Cardoso himself pointed out that, in reality, Brazil long ago encountered this political fragmentation and has already, essentially, become a post-party system. Most recent presidents and their parties, he notes, have received only around 20 percent of the popular vote in elections; once in power they can govern only by forging transactional alliances with the thirty-odd other parties in the legislature.

The emergence of so-called "pop-up parties" in the Netherlands is highly indicative of this dynamic. Because the Dutch have an extreme version of a proportional electoral system, any party that garners at least 0.067 of the popular vote gets a seat in the parliament. In 2017 no fewer than twenty-eight parties, most of them miniscule organizations that came into existence around particular issues such as immigration and aid to Ukraine, competed on the ballot in that small country of less than 17 million people.[27]

As touched upon earlier, France was ruled in the twentieth century by two large parties, alternatively or in cohabitation with each other. That all changed in 2017 when Emmanuel Macron, an independent who belonged to no party, won the presidency. He reached out directly to the public without a party apparatus, sidestepping the governing elites, but in his case with mainstream, pro-European instead of anti-European ideas. Donald Trump's election in the United States was the result of a populist end run around the Republican establishment, which rallied around him only after he won the nomination—yet which, even in victory, was unable to find enough unity within its ranks to accomplish its central campaign promise of rolling back Obamacare. The Brexit vote confounded all pollsters by rejecting calls for restraint by both of the main political parties, Labor and Conservative, as well as established experts and pundits.

As also noted earlier, in the 2017 elections in Germany, the two largest parties, Angela Merkel's Christian Democratic Union and the Social Democrats, had their worst showing of the entire post–World War II era, while an anti-immigrant nationalist party won enough seats to enter the Bundestag.

Italy has similarly splintered, with the populist parties of the far right and far left and some combination of both having turned the traditional centrist parties into historical relics. Indeed, the most interesting experiment in democracy taking place today is in Italy, where the internet-based Five Star Movement (FSM) garnered the largest block of votes in the March 2018 parliamentary elections. While the FSM suffers from what ails most populist movements in its simplistic approach to complex issues, it has nonetheless invented new forms of citizen engagement that should be closely watched.

Davide Casaleggio, who manages the FSM's online platform, explained the movement's success in *The WorldPost*: "Our experience is proof of how the Internet has made the established parties, and the previous organizational model of democratic politics more generally, obsolete and uneconomic."[28] Financed by online microdonations, the FSM, Casaleggio notes, spent only 9 cents per vote in the recent elections, compared with $8.50 by the mainstream parties. "The platform that enabled the success of the Five Star Movement is called Rousseau," he explains, "named after the 18th century philosopher who argued politics should reflect the general will of the people. And that is exactly what our platform does: it allows citizens to be part of politics. Direct democracy, made possible by the Internet, has given a new centrality to citizens and will ultimately lead to the deconstruction of the current political and social organizations. Representative democracy—politics by proxy—is gradually losing meaning."[29]

Following the slogan "Participate, don't delegate," the Five Star Movement has also developed software that allows citizens to propose laws directly. Its further plans include using blockchain technology to secure online voting and building an academy that will ensure training and "meritocratic selection" of candidates.

While political parties have splintered in Western political cultures that extol individual liberty above all, they have retained some measure of their clout not only in one-party China but in Japan as well. Both are large, populous countries in which the conformist or authoritarian streak in their culture surely plays a role. Here, partisanship would seem to bow before the weighty presence of a unifying civilizational identity.

The most reliable forecast is that relatively cogent parties will remain as agencies of collective political will wherever the cultural underpinning remains more solid. Elsewhere the fragmentation will be more pronounced. This bifurcation among polities will itself become a factor in the stability and continuity of relations among nations.

THINKING OUTSIDE THE BALLOT BOX

What is needed going forward is a new set of practices and institutions that can engage a reawakened public, which now has the tools to make its demands known and the political means through direct democracy to effect their realization. The challenge, we contend, lies in embracing and encouraging participation while avoiding populism. Democracy works best when the concerns of the public are proactively solicited on an ongoing basis, not passively provided in periodic elections in which organized special interests tend to hold the most sway. Popular concerns must then be absorbed and formulated by governing elites into sound, responsive policies presented back to the public itself in ballot measures (or to their representative legislatures in the bills) for approval, thus avoiding the buildup of resentment that leads to the kind of populist eruptions by the "left behind" we've seen with Brexit, Trump, and the rise of the anti-elite movements across Europe. For the Generation 89 Initiative, one of Europe's most vibrant and forward-looking organization of millennials, strengthening the European Citizens' Initiative, whereby laws are voted on directly, is one of its main proposals aimed at frustrating populism, which its supporters see as arising because the avenues of public agency have been blocked by the insider establishment. They believe that the connectivity of social networks, combined with this direct-democracy mechanism, will enable greater citizen participation in shaping the continent's future and legitimizing the European Union.[30]

In this new era we need to think outside the ballot box to create nonpartisan mediating institutions—islands of good faith, expertise, and experience insulated from the short-term, special-interest, and passionate influences of electoral systems—that can bridge polarized forces through the enlightened practices of reason, dialogue, negotiation, and compromise. Democratic discourse is not possible without a baseline of consensual truth that such institutions would strive to establish.

To be legitimate, such new institutions must be encompassing, impartial, and *disinterested* in the sense that they are not dominated by any one interest or set of interests to the exclusion of others. The best way to achieve this end is through a constitutional design that offsets both representative government and participation through more direct democracy with deliberative practices and institutions that provide a corrective ballast of knowledge and sober judgment to the raw expression of popular sovereignty. Such an arrangement would also be a counterweight to the fetish of elections for representatives, which in reality express the will not so much of the public as of organized special interests that have the time and resources to dominate the process.

In short, the structural response to the anger, alienation, and cynicism leading to the suicide of democracies is not more democracy of the same kind with only a change of partisan players. The response must involve going back to the drawing board of democratic design to update how it all works in a world far removed from its origins. The quantity and quality of the actors has changed, but the principle of balancing popular initiative with reasoned reflection in governing institutions outlined by the American Founders remains a guide for the future. The principle of a governing equilibrium between the pure expression of popular will and institutions of delegated authority that refine and enlarge the perspective of common interest through reasoned reflection is still universally applicable.

BACK TO THE DRAWING BOARD OF
CONSTITUTIONAL DESIGN

There is no one solution to the manifold problems that have caused today's crisis of democracy. The concrete proposals we present here, drawn from the US experience, are, therefore, not *the* answer, but a contribution to an answer, a suggestion for how to think about the renovation of democracy.

Because of our own practical activities in California, our proposals for institutional design are grounded in the particular circumstances there, including the fact that the citizens' ballot initiative process is advanced and commonly used as a form of direct democracy. In the age of social networks and frustration with party politics, the kind of direct democracy with which California has had long experience will play an ever greater role in other states and nations.

Historically, institutional innovation in US governance has first arisen in the states. Early constitution writing in the states following independence from Great Britain in 1776 informed the design of the US Constitution ratified in 1789. The next major innovations came a century later when direct democracy and professional management of government were introduced by the Progressive movement. Today, the states are once again the laboratories of democracy in the present US crisis. As before, institutional innovation in governance will come from the bottom up. How such change will be transmuted to the national level in the United States is a question beyond the scope of our experience and of this book. Our effort here is to focus on the fundamental features of democratic theory and practice that must find their own form at the national level.

THE AMERICAN FOUNDERS:
A REPUBLIC, NOT A DEMOCRACY

As noted, the first turn of US democracy was the ratification of the Constitution in 1789, after robust debate over the principles of governance and their practical application as experienced in the states in the decade after independence in 1776. This period of weak union under the Articles of Confederation, in which direct popular government in some states led to civil strife and fiscal instability, prompted the delegates to the Constitutional Convention to seek a more stable and enduring set of institutions in a more tightly bound nation.

Just as today we draw on the early reflections of James Madison or John Adams, the Founders in their day turned for guidance to the ancient histories of Greek democracy and the Roman republic. For the Founders, as the prominent Virginia revolutionary Patrick Henry wrote, the classical world was "the lamp of experience."[31]

What that lamp taught the Founders would surprise most twenty-first-century Americans. The word *democracy* did not appear in any of the early state constitutions. It does not appear in the US Constitution, or in the Bill of Rights or the Declaration of Independence. That is because America's constitutional architects not only distrusted democracy but, based on their close reading of Greek and Roman history, were actually hostile to the notion that it was the best system for governing society. James Madison, one of the authors of the Federalist Papers and the fourth US president, famously declared: "Democracy is the most vile form of government ... democracies have ever been spectacles of turbulence and contention; have ever been found incompatible with personal security or the rights of property; and have in general been as short in their lives as they have been violent in their deaths."[32] John Adams, the second American president, wrote: "Democracy never lasts long. It soon wastes, exhausts and murders itself. There never was a democracy yet that did not commit suicide.[33]"

These early American leaders came to such harsh conclusions about democracy through their avid study of Polybius, who lived during the last days of the Roman republic (200–118 BC), as well as a further recounting of Polybius and others by the Florentine Renaissance political theorist Machiavelli, who wrote his *Discourses on Livy* in 1517. Both Polybius and Machiavelli concluded that the best form of governance had always been a balanced mix of the monarchy, or executive power; aristocracy, the rule of the few; and democracy, the rule of the many. None of these forms in isolation, they argued, could produce long-lasting stability. Pure monarchy would inexorably degenerate into tyranny, aristocracy into oligarchy, and democracy into mob rule. Only when each watched over the others with reciprocal accountability could an enduring equilibrium be established. A constitutional republic designed along these lines—albeit with "natural aristoi" of talent, as Thomas Jefferson put it, instead of an aristocracy based on lineage or wealth[34]—provided the only way to curb the predatory appetites whetted when too much power is concentrated in any one place. What history and their own experience taught the Founders is that circuit breakers are needed to cut off power when too much of it flows to one set of interests—including, and especially, the electoral majority.

Taking into account this central lesson of antiquity, first in the states and then for the nation, the Framers instead designed a mixed constitutional republic that, while rooted in consent of the governed, delegated authority to elites—representative, indirectly elected or appointed bodies—that could "refine and enlarge the public views" as a counterweight against the popular passions of prejudice and the narrow horizons of self-interested constituencies.

For the Founders, popular sovereignty unchecked by the cool and reasoned deliberation of the meritorious few would invite majoritarian intolerance of individual and minority rights and, as occurred in antiquity, degenerate into mob rule and, in turn, summon tyranny to restore order. "No political truth is certainly of greater intrinsic value," Madison wrote in Federalist No. 47.[35]

For constitutional architects like John Adams, one way to achieve this check and balance was a bicameral legislature, each house of which having a distinct nature, as he first outlined in the spring of 1776 when he was asked by the North Carolina Provincial Congress to provide suggestions for a new government and constitution.

One house, according to Adam's design, would be a directly elected representative assembly that "should be in miniature an exact portrait of the people at large. It should think, feel and reason like them." Yet, he feared, such an assembly, by itself, would be "liable to all the vices, follies and frailties of an individual; subject to the fits of humor, starts of passion, flights of enthusiasm, partialities or prejudice, and consequently productive of hasty results and absurd judgments." Thus, he added, "all these errors ought to be corrected and defects supplied by some controlling power." If the immediate and parochial interests and passions of the people were to be reflected in a house of assemblymen, Adams reasoned, then an upper house, or senate fashioned on the Roman model, needed to be interposed. "A people cannot be long free, nor ever happy, whose government is in one assembly," he wrote. As an upper house, he envisioned a "distinct assembly" of "say twenty or thirty men" who "should have a free and independent exercise of judgment." Unlike the lower house, this upper house would not be directly accountable to the electorate, but appointed; its mandate would be to look out for the long-term common good, providing dispassionate, sober deliberation on legislation proposed by the lower house. Above all, it would buffer public passions of the moment and protect the stability and continuity of a law-based state.[36]

Senators, the delegates to the upper house, were to embody "the wisdom and foresight of persons" who were learned, well-informed, and contemplative and who could draw on "a long acquaintance with the history and manners of mankind."[37] Or, as Hamilton wrote in his notes on the Greek historian Plutarch's *Lives*, "The Senate was to the commonwealth what ballast is to a ship."[38] Madison similarly called a senate a necessary "anchor against popular fluctuations."[39]

In turn, checks would also have to be put in place to prevent a selected, or indirectly elected, senate from turning into a privileged aristocracy as it did in Roman times. It was out of this worry over incipient aristocracy that, by the 1840s, most states succumbed to the siren call of the democratic temper and implemented direct popular election of the upper houses as well as the assemblies, thus erasing the essential differences in function that Adams thought necessary.

South Carolina senator John C. Calhoun, sometimes referred to as the last Founding Father because he came along in the 1840s, decades after the US Constitution was drafted, felt compelled in the face of this tidal shift from a republican to a democratic sensibility to reinforce the distinction between the two. Calhoun saw that the ongoing expansion of suffrage and direct election of both the upper and the lower house of the legislature, now being proposed at the national level, would grant decisive power to a numerical majority instead of what he called a "concurrent majority." A concurrent majority entailed agreement between the distinct qualities of a deliberative, indirectly elected Senate and a directly elected House, whose majoritarian claims the Senate was designed to restrain and balance. Calhoun laid out the logic of his thinking in *A Disquisition on Government*,[40] a book written over six years, from 1843 to 1849 and published posthumously in 1851.

For Calhoun, the whole point of a mixed constitutional republic was "to prevent any one interest, or combination of interests, from using the powers of government to aggrandize itself at the expense of the others." The notion that "nothing more is necessary than suffrage" extended to all (male) citizens was thus at odds with what Calhoun called "the appropriate organism" that would not only express the will of the majority but embrace the interests of the entire society. In this way, he wrote, "the numerical majority instead of being the people, is only a portion of them." For Calhoun, majority rule registered at the ballot box wrongly assumed an identity with all interests in society. As he put it, rule solely by a democratic majority in both legislative houses meant the separation of power was only "nominal."[41] The imposition of limitations and restraints, what Calhoun called "the negative," is what prevents the majority from absolute domination. "It is, indeed, the negative which makes the constitution—and the positive which makes the government. The one is the power of acting and the other the power of preventing or arresting action. The two, combined, make constitutional government."[42] The success of ancient Rome, Calhoun noted, was due precisely to the establishment of the tribunes to represent the plebeians, and thus become a "negative" on the aristocratic Senate, and vice versa. It was the balance between the two that cemented the "bond of concord and harmony." When that balance fell into disequilibrium, the republic collapsed.

To be sure, Calhoun's disquisition on "the science of government" was not only grounded in his learned reading of the history of republics and his view of how societies worked in real life; they also reflected his concern that the slaveholding South was being subjugated by the more populous North, which was growing rapidly with the advent of textile mills and other early sprouts of industrialization.

The point of Calhoun's disquisition valuable for this book is that the same incipient democratic spirit that properly resisted making the upper house into a forum of aristocratic privilege or a bastion of slaveowning southerners also slowly eroded its republican function as a "distinct" body meant to check the immediate enthusiasms, interests, and passions of any given electoral majority at any given time.

In the decades following ratification of the Constitution, the expansion of suffrage to all white males (if not yet women, black people, or most American Indians) led to the emergence of political parties—the very "factions" the Framers so disdained—as a means to organize (and manipulate) all those new voters. "By a faction," James Madison wrote in Federalist No. 10, "I understand a number of citizens, whether amounting to a majority or a minority of the whole, who are united and actuated by some common impulse of passion, or of interest, adverse to the rights of other citizens, or to the permanent and aggregate interests of the community."[43] To the Framers' minds, republican mixed government was designed not only to buffer the immediate popular will of a democratic electorate but also as a "disinterested" way of governing that would thwart the efforts of factions or parties to band together across branches in order to impose their will and upset the institutional equilibrium.

Factions organized to mobilize partisan constituencies inevitably sought to dominate the public discourse through connections and money, consolidating into "machines" that disenfranchised average citizens who were not part of the patronage network. Expansion of the number of voters, in effect, tended to empower rather than diminish factional influence precisely because the electorate became so vast that only those who had the time, money, and interest to organize it could gain power.

Paradoxically, then, the expanded franchise led to the disempowerment of the individual voter in favor of organized special interests. What legal scholar Ganesh Sitaraman points out in *The Crisis of the Middle Class Constitution* (2017) was already true when the voter franchise was first widely extended: "Because of the asymmetry of time and resources, elections are dominated by the organized and the moneyed who are then chosen to govern. Elections even favor the rise of aristocracy."[44]

By the end of the nineteenth century, much like today, the disruptions of technological change and frustration with the capture of representative democracy by organized special interests fomented a populist revolt.

THE PROGRESSIVES: DIRECT DEMOCRACY AND SMART GOVERNMENT

By the turn of the twentieth century the United States had rebounded from the Civil War's devastation as a unified nation with a single market that was experiencing a great burst of commerce and economic growth. Railroads and telecommunications lines began to lace the nation. Modern public opinion was born with the dissemination of mass-circulation newspapers. The Industrial Revolution attracted mass migration to the cities where new manufacturing enterprises flourished. The self-reliant family farm that had for so long been the bedrock of the country's economy and political institutions introduced mechanization and became reliant on middlemen to sell crops in volatile markets. Henry Ford was gearing up his newfangled assembly line to produce automobiles. The first great skyscrapers rose in Chicago and New York to house the banking, railroad, mining, and oil monopolies that dominated voracious economic expansion. The superrich openly displayed a swank and frivolity so at odds with the traditional American qualities of frugality and modesty that Mark Twain awarded the era its own appellation, the "Gilded Age."[45]

As always in history, the creation of vast new wealth with new technologies brought new inequalities, new winners and losers, and new social movements that aimed to correct social injustice. New methods and patterns of production introduced whole new sets of concerns, from wages and working hours to food safety, energy and transportation costs, environmental protection, property use zoning, and urban housing shortages and blight. All these developments raced well ahead of regulation. Dwarfed by the changes in industry and commerce, government, then still small, tended to go with the flow. Well-greased political machines catered to the most powerful interests, settling on short-term fixes demanded by electoral cycles and the interests that had captured them. Government was increasingly seen as enabling the gilded few to get rich at the expense of the many. This ran against the majoritarian and egalitarian spirit of ordinary Americans. Partisan politicians lacked both the spine and the competence to manage the complexities of mass society in the emergent industrial era.

The social movements that arose to secure popular interests had a ready weapon for pushing back. The previous century's gradual turn toward a more expansive democracy had fortified the idea of one person, one vote. If representatives who were supposed to rule "for the people" had betrayed the public interest, then giving more power to the people themselves through direct democracy would fix the problem. In an age of mass communication through newspapers, after all, the ever-more-literate public could be as well informed in their decisions as their elected representatives. Representatives were no longer needed to "refine" the public view. All that was necessary was to remove the corrupt intermediaries or go around them by letting the people make laws directly at the ballot box. Meanwhile, to support elected officials with the knowledge and wisdom needed to lead, a major new concept of reform arose: banishing patrons and cronies and putting the management of government into the hands of nonpartisan experts and professionals. It was this philosophy that would animate the most far-reaching redesign in the institutions of government, especially at the state level, since the nation's founding.

The period of this movement (mainly 1890–1920) came to be known as the Progressive Era, a counterpoint to the Gilded Age. At the state level it was led by governors such as Robert M. La Follette of Wisconsin and Hiram Johnson of California. Legendary figure Hazen Pingree, then Detroit mayor and later Michigan governor, railed in 1899 against "the industrial slavery of trusts" while lowering street car fares, fixing the sewer system, and proposing municipal ownership of utilities.[46]

The depression of the 1890s had given rise to the so-called Populist movement. Some historians see Populism as the precursor to the Progressive movement with its call for more direct democracy, social justice, and women's suffrage—but others view it as Progressivism's antithesis because of its distrust of urban elites, its intermittent racial intolerance and anti-Semitism, and its backward-looking agricultural "utopianism" on the cusp of the Industrial Age. From today's standpoint, the Populists were not unlike a combination of the anti-elitist politics of Donald Trump and Bernie Sanders.[47] The Populists, mainly driven by the interests of small farmers, forged alliances in some places with labor unions. By contrast, the Progressive movement was largely rooted in the urban, educated middle class.

Both Populists and Progressives were drawn to the notion of discontented constituencies asserting their interests through an entirely new mechanism of voter sovereignty that bypassed representative government. Specifically, the Progressives envisioned a system in which checks on the state legislatures and big-city bosses would come from below—the people themselves in their collective wisdom.

To strengthen majority rule registered directly by the public, the Progressives favored several instruments. The first was the citizen ballot initiative, imported from Switzerland, where it had been implemented in the late nineteenth century. It allowed members of the public to propose and pass laws, as well as amend state constitutions, without going through the legislature. The Progressives also favored the referendum process, allowing the public to vote to amend or overturn laws passed by the legislature, and the "recall," whereby elected officials with whom voters had become unhappy could be removed from office. Some even supported a recall by referendum for the independent, appointed judiciary.

The Progressives well understood that the direct democracy they espoused would have been anathema to Founders like Adams and Madison, and that it was against the very spirit of mixed government enshrined in the federal constitution. But in their view, history had proved Adams and Madison wrong: the republican experiment had foundered and decayed into a system that enabled and protected the privileged few.

In other ways, the Progressives embraced the Framers ideals. To establish "disinterested" governance, Progressives proposed to delegate authority to nonpartisan experts, independent of politics and insulated from elections, who would regulate business and administer cities and states whose populations were swelling. Railroad and utility commissions were born in this period, as were professional city managers. The kind of independent, appointed regulatory bodies established in those days now exist all across the United States. To take one example, the Railroad Commission of Texas, that state's first regulatory commission, was established in 1891. Today its mandate is to oversee the oil and gas industry. Commissions that regulate public utilities are common in all states now.

A craze for the initiative, referendum, and recall swept the states, especially the newer, western states where party machines that opposed such measures were weaker, population less concentrated, and the hated monopolies, particularly railroad and mining companies, more dominant.

Each state tailored its reforms to the particular abuses being addressed at the time. In Oregon the target was the undue influence of corrupt political machines. In California, Governor

Hiram Johnson, who was elected in 1911, barnstormed the state in a successful campaign to harness voter ire at the Southern Pacific Railroad's hold on the state legislature.

States often took cues on the substance of reforms from the most prominent Progressive of the day, Governor Robert "Fighting Bob" La Follette of Wisconsin, who was elected to two terms starting in 1900.[48] La Follette showed the way by legislating direct primaries, civil service reform, a graduated income tax, and a ban on political contributions by commercial interests. He and his Progressive allies also enacted conservation laws, railroad and insurance company regulation through independent commissions, a statewide system of worker's compensation, and regulations regarding child labor. Theodore Roosevelt remarked that Wisconsin had become "literally a laboratory for wise, experimental legislation aiming to secure the social and political betterment of the people as a whole."[49]

Most broadly conceived, what La Follette contributed to the Progressive agenda was the practice of smart government enlightened by knowledge to match the growing complexity of mass industrial society. According to the "Wisconsin idea," as his approach came to be known, efficient government required control of institutions by voters rather than special interests, and the involvement of legal and economic specialists and social and natural scientists would produce the most effective government. The governor enlisted experts from the University of Wisconsin faculty to consult with legislators and help draft many of the state's groundbreaking laws, including tax reforms, public regulation of utilities, and the nation's first workers' compensation law.[50] Summing up later in the century, Adlai Stevenson II, the eloquent liberal governor and presidential candidate from Illinois, remarked: "The Wisconsin tradition meant more than a simple belief in the people. It also meant a faith in the application of intelligence and reason to the problems of society. It meant a deep conviction that the role of government was not to stumble along like a drunkard in the dark, but to light its way by the best torches of knowledge and understanding it could find."[51]

The novel idea of bringing the best and brightest into government as a way to supplant politicized administration gained wide appeal in the wake of the partisan bickering, corruption, and cronyism that led up to the Progressive Era. As the powerful reformist columnist Walter Lippmann later wrote, "The value of expert mediation is not that it sets up opinion to coerce the partisans, but that it disintegrates partisanship."[52]

The reformist ferment in the states percolated up to the national level. In response to rising anger against discriminatory rates by the railroad monopolies, the Interstate Commerce Commission was established as early as 1887, and the Sherman Anti-trust Act was passed in 1890. The Pure Food and Drug Act was enacted in 1906, the first permanent national income tax in 1913, and the first federal child labor laws in 1916. Thanks to Teddy Roosevelt's advocacy in his 1912 presidential campaign, direct primaries were adopted across the nation. The Constitution itself changed: the Seventeenth Amendment was added in 1911, establishing the direct election of the US Senate, and the Nineteenth Amendment, ratified in 1920, expanded suffrage to include women.[53]

In short, the expansion of democracy went hand in hand with the expansion of government as US economic growth, driven by technological innovations such as the steam engine, electricity, and the automobile, took off and mass industrial society took hold. The idea that a government controlled more closely by the voters and administered by nonpartisan experts could enhance public well-being signaled a historic shift from the concept that limiting the scope of government and the reach of democracy was the best protection of liberty.

THE THIRD TURN: PARTICIPATION WITHOUT POPULISM

Today, heading toward the midpoint of the twenty-first century, America is facing a crisis of governance not dissimilar to that at the turn of the twentieth century. The financial crash of 2008–9 exposed deep fissures in the social and economic status quo. Globalization and rapid technological changes have generated deep insecurity over job losses and diminishing opportunities for upward mobility. Digital capitalism has created new information monopolies and, along with the explosion of finance, concentrated wealth in the top 5 percent. Polarization and partisan gridlock have sharply divided the country, disabling the capacity to achieve a governing consensus and paralyzing government. The "swamp" of special interests has largely taken over state capitols and Washington, DC.

In sum, greater democracy alone has not fixed the problems of democracy. As Alexis de Tocqueville warned in his observations of Americans in the 1830s: "I hold it to be sufficiently demonstrated that universal suffrage is by no means a guarantee of the wisdom of the popular choice. Whatever its advantages may be, this is not one of them." [54] Certainly, the time is as ripe now as it was in the Progressive Era for a new turn in American democracy. Taking into account the lessons of the first two turns, the third renovation would link the Progressive ideas of direct democracy and delegation of authority to knowledgeable nonpartisan elites with the Founders' belief in the deliberative ballast of an upper legislative house insulated from direct elections. In short, a mixed constitution that encourages participation but not populism, mediated by practices and institutions that foster consensus. As in the previous turns of American democracy, this one will be built from the bottom up, in the states.

Designing new institutions for the coming era first requires an understanding of the flaws of direct democracy. These are most evident in California, where the citizen ballot initiative dominates governance. In fact, it is often called the fourth branch of government.

The Fate of the Citizen Ballot Initiative

Even at the height of the Progressive Era, direct democracy did not deliver consistently on its promise to advance society. In 1914 voters in California, Colorado, Oregon, and Washington rejected ballot initiatives to adopt the eight-hour workday. In that same year, voters in Ohio, Missouri, and Nebraska rejected proposals for women's suffrage.[55] Organized special interests quickly learned to game the system, manipulating the people's sovereignty by placing deceptive propositions on the ballot that would accomplish the opposite of their perceived intent. In 1912, for example, the Colorado Iron and Fuel Company, owned by John D. Rockefeller, sponsored a noble-sounding initiative that promised to limit the length of the workday for miners; in reality, if the initiative had passed, it would have gutted a stricter measure passed by the legislature.[56]

Similar ills plague the citizen ballot initiative system today. In 2010, Proposition 23 in California qualified for the ballot under the title "The California Jobs Initiative." It was in fact sponsored by out-of-state oil companies; its hidden aim was to undo legislation to curb fossil fuel emissions that cause climate change, laws whose strictures the companies feared would spread to other states. Opponents labeled it the "Dirty Energy Proposition." Ultimately defeated, it turned out to be the most expensive ballot initiative battle in the state's history, with the pro and con sides together spending a total of $78.4 million.[57]

Citizen ballot initiatives remain vulnerable to such abuses because they entail huge effort and expense. Merely to qualify a proposition for the ballot in California requires its sponsors to gather hundreds of thousands of voter signatures. The required number is based on previous voter turnout; in 2016 that meant 365,000 signatures were needed to put a proposed law on the ballot, and 585,407 to put forward a proposed amendment to the state constitution.[58] Unsurprisingly, collecting signatures has become a business in itself. In any given electoral season in California, paid signature gatherers abound outside supermarkets and other public places.

In the California election season of 2016, so many initiatives were competing to qualify that the average cost of acquiring signatures soared to $5 apiece, an all-time high. At that rate, some $1.8 million would be required to put a proposed law on the ballot, and $2.9 million for a proposed constitutional amendment. Such princely sums are merely the ante: they do not take into account the money needed to fund, in effect, a full-blown election campaign to get the measure passed or to defeat it. Citizen involvement is further marginalized by the professionalization of campaign consulting and the employment of the persuasion industry of public relations.[59]

Money determines not only the capacity to sponsor an initiative but also the power to block it. In 2018, soft drink companies qualified a ballot initiative that would have required a two-thirds vote by localities on any tax or fee increase. Their aim was to prevent a tax on their sugary sodas. To prevent what would have been the devastation of local government finances, the legislature passed a law prohibiting a soda tax until 2030, and the ballot measure was withdrawn. When Governor Jerry Brown signed the bill, he called it "extortion." In 2016, when California real estate developers feared that a measure would qualify that would have hiked taxes on commercial property, they raised $30 million to campaign against it. Daunted by the prospect of a ruinously expensive battle, the sponsors decided not to go forward. As early as 2009, then–chief justice of the California Supreme Court Ron George expressed his concern about the power of money, but with even deeper reservations. He asked, "Has the voter initiative now become the tool of the very type of special interests it was intended to control, and an impediment to the effective functioning of a true democratic process?"

If there is any doubt about the peril to its integrity that the citizen ballot initiative faces, an investigation in 2016 by the *New York Times* reported that corporate, union, and other organized special interests have discovered where the new power lies in an era when other public institutions and politicians have lost the public trust.[60] Their aim now is to influence the election officials who write the ballot arguments that can sway voters one way or the other. In most of the twenty-six states that have ballot initiatives, the summary arguments are written by the secretary of state. In California, that person is the attorney general.[61]

Subversion by special interests is hardly the only weakness that dogs the ballot initiative process. These initiatives sometimes embody the darker impulses of the voters themselves—as when majoritarian sentiments expressed through direct democracy violate the rights of minorities. Such was the case with both California Proposition 22 in 2000 and Prop 8 in 2008, which sought to outlaw same-sex marriage. Both succeeded at the polls, but were later overturned on appeal by the California Supreme Court.

Perhaps the greatest danger for intelligent governance comes from the unintended consequences of well-meaning ballot initiative measures based on the public's short-term horizons and momentary obsessions that would have been filtered out if passed through a deliberative process. And California has no requirement that a majority of eligible voters turn up at the polls. If a majority of the 20 percent who show up on Election Day vote to change the state's constitution, then that's what happens.[62] In other words, even an unrepresentative minority or plurality can dictate the law to all citizens of the state.

Undeliberated policymaking through the citizen ballot initiative in California, especially in fiscal matters, has led to a cascade of cumulative consequences that have tied governance in knots. It has tended to lock in spending and lock out revenues while perpetuating an obsolete tax system completely divorced from the real economy.

Proposition 13, the famous 1978 anti-tax measure that severely limited the property tax, set off the cascade of misguided policies. It led to other propositions over succeeding years to compete and compensate for the dearth of funds, including measures put forward by the powerful teacher's union which, through a ballot measure, secured 40 percent of the general fund budget for K–14 education at the expense of the public universities, public pensions, and other social needs such as the state's MediCal services for the poor. The public's resistance to taxing themselves for all these state needs led to decades of mounting debts and deficits that left California by 2010 on the brink of bankruptcy. To avoid that fate, the public was willing to raise income taxes only on the rich, which in turn made the budget perilously volatile because it became poised on a very narrow base: by 2017, income taxes provided nearly 70 percent of state revenues, the top 1 percent paid 50 percent of incomes taxes, and only 15,000 people paid half of that. When cyclical recession hits and the capital gains and incomes of the rich diminish, so do the tax revenues. Thus, programs funded in a flush period must be drastically cut during a downturn. When the 2008–9 financial crisis shaved 3 percent of the state's GDP, tax revenues dropped 23 percent.

In short, since each successive fiscal fix at the ballot box was short-term and piecemeal, direct democracy deepened the dysfunction of state government instead of improving the situation.

The same kind of counterproductive dynamic of direct democracy afflicts the criminal justice system in California. Voters with the good intention of curbing violent crime through mandating prison sentences at the ballot box instead of in the courts ended up creating a situation in which the state spends as much on prisons as higher education.[63]

That government by initiative is so dysfunctional is no surprise. As the Public Policy Institute for California noted in its October 2012 report "Improving California's Democracy," less than 10 percent of all voters polled—Democrats, Republican, and Independents—said that they want the governor and legislature to make the tough choices involved in the state budget, while a full 80 percent said California's voters should make those decisions through the initiative process. Yet only one in five voters said they know a lot about how state and local governments spend and raise money, and most "cannot name the largest area of state spending (K–14 education) or the largest area of state revenues (personal income taxes)."[64]

Direct democracy in California had gone so awry that in 2011 *The Economist* published a cover story on the initiative process titled "Where It All Went Wrong: A Special Report on California's Dysfunctional Democracy." In that issue, *The Economist* editorialized, "The initiative culture in California today may resemble James Madison's worst nightmare. Passions are inflamed instead of cooled. Confrontation replaces compromise as minority factions (special interests) battle one another with rival initiatives."[65] The eminent publication further declared that the state was "ungovernable" and served as a warning to "voters all over the world" of the excesses of "extreme democracy" embodied in the citizen ballot initiative.[66]

Despite the deep flaws illustrated by the California experience, the ideal of direct democracy remains lodged fondly in the hearts and minds of the voters. The challenge is not how to get rid of the citizen ballot initiative, but how to correct those flaws through new practices and institutions that make it a genuine avenue for change when corrupt or inattentive political elites and special interests capture representative government.

What the New Turn Looks Like

The correction for such flaws lies precisely in restoring the deliberative ballast of a strong mixed government held dear by the Founders. This can best be established by incorporating the Progressive innovation of delegating authority to accountable nonpartisan bodies with the knowledge and expertise required to govern in an ever-more-complex information society. Such an innovation, in conjunction with representative and direct democracy, would provide a smartening complement to the exploding multitude of plural voices and competing interests that has arisen with the participatory power of social media. Neither the direct rule of public passions nor rule by the sober minds of the best and brightest, alone and apart, is good for any republic. The most appropriate constitutional arrangement for governing the highly mobilized and networked societies of the future entails institutionalizing these two functions as a check and balance on each other.

The relevant question is how the wisdom of the American Founders might find institutional expression today. Is it possible to design a system of governance for the twenty-first century in which there is meaningful participation but not populism, and politics without money? If the public feel ignored by the status quo, can their concerns be heard and met before destabilizing populist narratives take shape? To achieve collective intelligence instead of opening governance to a "dumb mob," that hearing must be processed into considered policy, not merely reflected back in its raw, potentially explosive, and counterproductive form.

Because California is where the authors live and have been actively engaged, because with its $2.5 trillion economy and 40 million people California approximates a major nation-state, because the culture of California is famously open to change, that is where it has made the most sense for us to start putting the politics of renovation to work.

CALIFORNIA AS A LABORATORY OF DEMOCRACY

When citizen ballot initiatives are thoroughly deliberated and thought through by responsible civic organizations, they can improve governance instead of worsen it. Indeed, in the past decade heightened public frustration with endless partisan grid-lock and mounting debts and deficits led to passage of several key reform measures through ballot initiatives deployed not by organized special interests but by coalitions of citizens' groups backed by several of California's large nonprofit foundations. The foundations funded the research and staffing for the deliberative phase of discussing and formulating propositions. Then the citizen groups got their initiatives on the ballot, either by pressuring the governor and legislature to put them there by a vote in the legislature,[67] or by collecting the hundreds of thousands of signatures required to bypass the lawmakers. A coalition of organizations ranging from the NAACP and the American Association of Retired Persons (AARP) to the League of Women Voters and the Chamber of Commerce succeeded in passing a ballot initiative in 2008 that placed the power to draw voting districts with a citizens' commission instead of the legislature. In 2010 another initiative extended citizens' redistricting to congressional districts. As a result, partisan gerrymandering is no longer possible in California. Also in 2010 voters passed a measure sponsored by citizen groups, referred to the ballot by the legislature, and supported by Governor Schwarzenegger known as the Top Two Primaries Act. This act established nonpartisan state primaries in which the top two vote-getters, no matter their party affiliation, would face off in the general election. The idea was that instead of marking out extreme positions to consolidate a partisan base, candidates would now have an incentive to appeal to the broad moderate middle of the electorate.

Yet another measure, passed by frustrated voters in 2010, sought to end partisan legislative gridlock by reducing from two-thirds to a simple majority the votes needed to pass budgets.

While each of these measures helped relieve immediate problems paralyzing the state, they did not go the distance in creating a twenty-first-century deliberative platform for building consensus concerning California's long-term future and effective ways to get there. Our aim is to institutionalize the process in order to mitigate abuse and misguided efforts while ensuring that public participation through the ballot initiatives will also result in good policy.

To that end, in 2010 we founded the Think Long Committee for California, a bipartisan group composed of "eminent, experienced, and disinterested" citizens to ponder long-term solutions to the state's enduring problems, including rebooting the relationship between representative and direct democracy through a new "civic software." Though steeped in public affairs from their experience over the years, none of the members we recruited actively represented any constituency or interest group. All set aside whatever partisan identity they were associated with in order to engage the big picture as we convened each month for a year at Google headquarters in Mountain View, California.[68]

By the end of 2012 the Think Long Committee produced a full set of recommendations, the "Blueprint to Renew California," that laid out the reform agenda it would seek to implement over the coming years. Its three main proposals were to (a) reform the initiative process to make it more deliberative, transparent, and flexible; (b) stabilize budget volatility; and (c) raise new revenue to sustainably finance public higher education and infrastructure through modernizing the tax code to reflect the service and information character of the state's twenty-first-century economy.

The central proposal, consistent with the arguments of this book, was to establish a nonpartisan deliberative body appointed by the governor and legislative leadership with the power to vet ballot initiatives and to propose its own well-considered initiatives to the public without the step of gathering signatures.

Appointees would be selected on a nonpartisan basis with staggered terms across electoral cycles to ensure no sitting governor or legislature can stack the membership. To cultivate a long-term perspective, terms would be similar to those for California State University trustees, which run for eight years. The stated purpose of this body, called the Citizens Council for Government Accountability, is to "consider the long-term public interest as a counterbalance to the short-term mentality and special interest political culture" that dominates state politics.[69] The lead proponent who crafted this proposal was Ronald George, who had served as chief justice of the California Supreme Court for fifteen years and had joined the Think Long Committee upon retirement.[70]

In a way, the Think Long Committee itself is a template for the very kind of deliberative body—insulated from the short-term horizon of the partisan election cycle and special interests—that ought to be institutionalized as part of the new constitutional balance we propose going forward.

Notwithstanding the prestige and thoughtfulness behind the idea, such a council will not be established in California overnight, but step-by-step. So far, Think Long has advanced the process by passing a bill in the legislature, backed by a coalition of thirty labor, business, and civil rights groups, that reformed the initiative process for the first time in eighty years. Governor Brown signed the bill—the Ballot Initiative Transparency Act—into law in April 2014. It requires public hearings to be held after 25 percent of the signatures required to qualify a measure are gathered. Further, it allows sponsors to make changes in their initial filing after those hearings and to negotiate compromises with the legislature and governor that take into account unintended consequences. And it allows sponsors to withdraw the original initiative altogether if a compromise is reached to introduce legislation that satisfies the sponsors' aims without resorting to the pubic ballot. The measure further requires a public listing on the website of the secretary of state of organizations and persons who are financing the pro and con positions up to the day of an election.

The considerable impact of this reform was already felt in the 2016 election season when the governor and legislature reached a compromise with labor unions that had filed several separate and competing ballot initiatives; as a result, a law was passed upping the minimum wage in scheduled steps to $15 an hour by 2020. In 2018, an initiative that would give consumers control over their personal data forced the big-tech companies to the negotiating table with the legislature. As a result of the compromise between Silicon Valley and privacy advocates, California passed the first digital privacy act in the United States, and the ballot measure was withdrawn.

FUNDAMENTAL REDESIGN OF STATE GOVERNMENT

Based on the experience of these intermediate reforms, it is possible to imagine a redesign of California's state government that would fully accomplish the "third turn" in American democracy at the state level: combining the Founders' deliberative corrective with the Progressives' direct democracy. It is a system that would remove big money from politics and bolster participation without populism.

The redesign would have two central pillars.

First, it would replace direct popular elections of state assembly members with an indirect "stepped" structure of representation harkening back to Thomas Jefferson's vision of government by human-scale "district republics."

Today, electoral districts may include millions of constituents. Candidates must raise correspondingly huge sums to pay for media buys, pollsters, and campaign strategists. If the districts were downsized to the human scale of large neighborhoods, and if elections were to become nonpartisan affairs as they are in many city councils today, this financial imperative would be eliminated and candidates could go back to people-to-people campaigning fortified by today's online tools.

In this scheme, delegates would be directly elected at a neighborhood council level to deal with issues in their own realm of life and competence. They would then, in turn, collectively choose representatives to the state assembly with broader responsibilities and a wider scope of competence. This upward pyramidal structure would be reversed in the administration and provision of services, wherein each delegate would become a local representative of the government at the neighborhood council level. In this way, those chosen to lead would also be directly accountable to their human-scale constituencies for effectively implementing the governing policies put in place on their behalf.

Here is how the system would work: California has a population nearing 40 million; in the present arrangement, the senate has 40 members, and the assembly 80. Both houses could be combined into a larger assembly of 120 representatives. By removing representational duplication in two houses, the average population size of election districts could be reduced from about 1 million each to 300,000. Each district of 300,000 could be further divided into six neighborhood districts of 50,000 people each. In addition to face-to-face contact in these smaller districts, new technologies similar to those employed in Massive Open Online Courses in education can easily tie together such a population in real-time interaction. Each of the six neighborhoods would elect a delegate; the delegates from the six neighborhoods would, in turn, elect one representative for the state level.

By reducing the number of electors at each level, the need for campaign financing to reach large constituencies would diminish almost completely. At this scale, the kind of online fundraising tools that empower small donors employed by the Five Star Movement in Italy could be the mechanism of choice in this kind of neighborhood elections.[71]

Above all, this new civic system would close the distance between the representative and the represented while involving individual citizens and diverse constituencies more meaningfully in elections in which their vote really matters.

As for the redesign's second pillar, with representative democracy organized in the stepped system just described, in which the present senate and assembly districts would be merged into one body, a new, nonpartisan senate comprising "eminent men and women of experience and expertise" would be selected in the following way:

- Elected county officials would band together in a population-balanced grouping of ten regions drawn from California's fifty-eight counties to appoint ten members.
- The state's higher education institutions—the University of California, the California State University System, and the community colleges—would each have one senator appointed by the respective chancellors or presidents, totaling three members.

- The governor would appoint six independent at-large members.
- The legislative leadership would also appoint six independent at-large members.

Nominating committees or conventions of constituents could be called in each case to recommend candidates to the appointing officials. Obviously, the number of appointees suggested here must be flexible and reflect the diverse makeup of the population. The central point is that appointments must be made by officials who are directly elected by the citizenry or who represent permanent institutional functions (e.g., public higher education) that are integral to the state's long-term health and development.

This new senate would incorporate the Citizens Council idea of the Think Long Committee—an impartial body that both vets and proposes ballot initiatives—into the traditional structure of a bicameral legislature. Having its members appointed instead of elected would insulate the new senate from the special-interest influences and short-term horizons of electoral politics, helping to ensure its independence and integrity. To foster a long-term perspective, the terms of office would be eight years, with appointments crossing electoral cycles and staggered to prevent the appointing officials from stacking the body in their favor.

The new body would also serve as a "permanent task force and think tank"—in essence, a kind of adjunct meritocracy—to refine and enlarge the public view through a long-term perspective with the capacity to see through the implementation of policies for years at a time without a break in continuity. In its function as a forward-looking think tank, the reconfigured senate would survey best practices and engage in modeling and research in order to inform its policy proposals. Well staffed, it would solicit public input through both open platforms and advanced scientific survey methods to determine public concerns not being addressed, or being addressed inadequately, by the elected legislature.

The revamped senate could employ innovative online e-deliberation tools pioneered by the Five Star Movement, such as Lex (the word for law in Latin) and Lex Iscritti. The Lex tool is used by members of the Italian parliament to share their legislative proposals for explanation, comment, and discussion by constituents. Lex Iscritti allows citizens themselves to make proposals to elected officials, from the bottom up, that can then be shaped into legislation through back-and-forth discussion.[72] Such input and feedback would be processed into thoroughly formulated policies presented back to the voter for consent through the direct democracy of ballot initiatives, which the senate would have the power to propose without going through the signature-gathering process, or by consent of the representative house through an up-or-down simple-majority vote of the both houses. To filter out the influence of lobbyists and special pleaders, no amendments would be allowed after the deliberative stage.

Because the senate is the formal sponsor of such legislation, it would be able to amend or update approved measures after they are passed by the public if those changes are consistent with the original purpose.

With these new functions, the senate would serve as a deliberative body not only for the "sober second reading" of legislation proposed by the representative assembly, *but also for the sober second reading and review of citizen ballot initiatives.* Thus popular sovereignty would have the final say in passing proposed legislation, but only after it had been formulated and thoroughly deliberated by a senate whose authority is delegated on the meritocratic basis of experience, judgment, and expertise. It is this mixed constitutional arrangement that would ensure both legitimacy and accountability to the "third turn" in American democracy.

Following the example of the Wisconsin idea of the Progressive Era, California's two large institutions of higher education—California State University and the University of California—ought to establish close research links with the revised senate so as to bring their considerable expertise in the social and physical sciences to bear on legislation and regulation. Such links to the legislature do not exist today, because the universities, understandably, do not want to become enmeshed in political agendas. A nonpartisan senate that is appointed and removed from electoral politics would assuage that concern.

Here is how the process might work in practice:

1. Through the online California Open Platform the state senate would solicit from the public the top five concerns not being addressed, or not being addressed adequately, by the legislature. Additional scientific opinion surveys would also be conducted to affirm that the results offered voluntarily are shared by the general public and not the result of activist or special interest campaigns.

   After a period of open comment and surveys, the senate would choose the top priority listed by voters and begin work developing a ballot measure to resolve the issue. Initiative measures developed by the senate should be few and far between, addressing only the most crucial issues and constitutional amendments.

If a ballot proposition has already been filed aimed at addressing the same concerns, the senate would review its provisions, assess whether it will achieve what it claims, suggest amendments as necessary if consistent with the purpose, and recommend for or against the proposition in any upcoming vote.

2. Let's say that the number-one priority listed by the public through the Open Platform is fixing the finances of the California State University (CSU) system, which has twenty-three campuses and 470,000 students. Since funding has dropped dramatically since the 2008–9 financial crisis, it faces a choice of turning away students or raising tuition to unaffordable rates.

3. To search for a solution, the senate conducts or commissions a modeling study of the California economy, employing the expertise of former state finance directors from both previous Republican and Democratic gubernatorial administrations, as well as the former economic forecaster of the state legislative analyst.

   No state office presently has this capacity. The governor's director of finance and the legislative analyst focus on the current year's budget, the Board of Equalization on tax collection. The comptroller signs the checks. Staff of the assembly members are devoted to their immediate agendas and their expertise is severely limited on statewide matters.

4. These analysts find that there is little further leeway in taxing the upper end of income, which already is the

highest in the United States. On the other hand, a sales tax on goods is highly regressive; the poor pay proportionately much more for goods than those with higher incomes.

What the analysts discover is that 80 percent of California's modern economic activity occurs in the service sector, barely any of it taxed except for welding and gift wrapping. Their modeling also shows that every 1 percent of tax on this large volume of activity generates $7 billion dollars annually—close to the annual budget of the entire CSU system. At the same time, the research team finds that many services, including those of lawyers, accountants, and architects, are largely discretionary and not used much by the state's less well-off citizens.

5. Based on this research, a senate working group proposes a ballot measure that would impose a 1 percent sales tax on services to adequately and sustainably fund the CSU system, bring down tuition costs, and ensure all qualified applicants can attend. The group calls its bill "One Penny for Higher Education for All." While recognizing that the well-off will pay more of this tax because they use more high-end services, the senate also notes that when it comes to funding public institutions that benefit all, everyone should have skin in the game.

6. Public hearings would invite stakeholders—taxpayer associations, student and faculty groups, parents and families, university trustees and administrators, employers who rely on CSU to find qualified workers, and the like—to comment on the proposed measure. The senate

would poll the general public as well. The measure would be tweaked as necessary to respond to public concerns not previously recognized.

7. The actual initiative, which under this plan the senate can directly place on the ballot without gathering signatures, would be quite simple, explaining the central role of public higher education in promoting upward mobility and calling for a dedicated stream of revenue, financed by the 1 percent service tax, that would enable the CSU to cut tuition while accepting all qualified applicants. Further, it would explain that the reliable income stream would also allow the CSU to collateralize borrowing for capital spending on earthquake retrofits and other infrastructure improvements to accord with the state's climate change regulations.

8. The one-page measure would be put to a public vote and indicate that, if it passed, the legislature would be directed to work out the intricacies and details of the bill—for example, a clause that would preclude the legislature from making this revenue stream a "ceiling" that would eliminate other necessary support from the state budget. Twenty pages of legalese that would be necessary to align the measure with state codes or to spell out collection procedures would prove too complex to be properly considered by the voting public.

9. Alternatively, if the elected assembly can muster the two-thirds vote required by state law to pass a tax increase, the measure could be withdrawn from the public ballot and pass as legislation.

10. If the ballot measure does not pass, the senate would have to return to the drawing board and devise a plan the public finds acceptable while still addressing the core issue. For example, it could move the parts around, reducing the sales tax on services to half a cent and dividing the other portion between a sales tax on goods and a further minimal increase on the rich.

Another issue that direct democracy mediated in this way could address is the state water plan. One extant proposal calls for digging two huge tunnels to bring water to Southern California from the north; other plans call for more conservation in the largest southern cities like Los Angeles and spreading water runoff into groundwater sinks as a cheaper and more environmentally sound approach—a proposal that may not cover all water supply needs. Each side resists the proposals of the other. Here, the senate could step in with a compromise—for example, one tunnel instead of two, combined with conservation measures crafted by a task force of the leading specialists on the matter in the state's universities. Since most Californians live in the south, but most water flows from the north—with vital agricultural zones in the middle—a statewide plan must work for all. An impartial body representing the state will be more able to come up with a fair plan than legislators beholden to southern water consumers, Central Valley farmers, or Northern California environmental activists. A comprehensive measure that shares the burden and benefits should then be put to a ballot measure vote of all the state's citizens.

The value of this process is that responsible policymakers in the senate, insulated from the electoral cycle and immediate constituency pressures while tasked with thinking long-term, would be able to step back, look at the big picture, and come up with a comprehensive plan and permanent fix that responds to a statewide public priority. They would have resolved a key issue for the state that the elected assembly did not tackle—because of election cycle fears over a tax increase, their own immediate local priorities, or their ingrained inclination toward quick fixes and short-term patches that only kick the can down the road.

The prospect of a selected, or indirectly elected, senate may seem wishful or nostalgic thinking in the context of the modern United States—a throwback to the postcolonial ideals of John Adams and other Founders long dead. Yet within the present experience of other major democracies are examples that make the idea less far-fetched. After all, both the German upper house, the Bundesrat, and the French Sénat are indirectly elected. The compelling value of a "distinct" deliberative upper house in a bicameral system is finding new appreciation in recent debates over the reform of the Canadian Senate, also an appointed, nonelected body.

Although Canada has half the gross domestic product (GDP) of California, it has roughly the same population. Its governor general (representing the Commonwealth) formally appoints the 105 members of the Senate on the advice of the prime minister. Those appointed are "eminent citizens," including former cabinet ministers and provincial governors who serve "life terms" up to the age of seventy-five, when they must retire. The terms average ten to twelve years. The criteria for senatorial appointments spelled out in the Canadian constitution include a candidate's independence, long-term perspective, professional and life experience, and home province (the last considered to achieve regional equality in accordance with federalism).

Recently, the youthful, vigorously reformist prime minister Justin Trudeau has sought to end the practice of appointments along party lines, and as sinecures rewarding old pols, in order to make the Canadian Senate the genuine nonpartisan body it was meant to be. To that end, he has also proposed the establishment of citizen assemblies that will gather to nominate candidates for the prime minister's office for appointment by the governor general.

The main purpose of the Canadian Senate is to serve as a "sober second chamber" for deliberation of legislative proposals made by the elected House of Commons. For legislation to pass, the Senate must concur with the House of Commons and is empowered to reject legislation. Because it has a strong committee structure and a long-term mandate, the upper chamber takes the time and makes the effort to produce extensive studies and reports that enable in-depth consideration and discussion of pending legislation, as well as to inform the drafting of new legislation in the House.

In the Canadian system, key legislation thus starts with a broad idea, then turns to knowledgeable, nonpartisan professionals and experts to translate the idea into a detailed practical program plan and budget; next the Senate holds an up-or-down vote on it. Canada's national health system, for example, began with the legislature crafting and approving an outline that was only several pages long, which was elaborated into a full-blown program by nonpartisan technical experts, and then presented back to the legislature for final approval. In the United States, by contrast, the Affordable Care Act ("Obamacare") began as a two-thousand-page monstrosity written by and for political and special interests, engendering political battles that are still stirring.

"As long as the Parliament remains the primary source of legitimacy," Trudeau told us, "the value of the unelected Senate is that it is insulated from the influence of electoral cycles and special interests and thus able to step back and take the long view." Like Trudeau, former prime minister Paul Martin values the distinct long-term perspective and think-tank capacity of the Senate, which he estimates is presently 70 percent "meritocratic" and 30 percent political. (The British House of Lords is also slowly but surely being transformed into a body that performs a similar long-term perspective and think-tank role. In April 2018 it released an advisory study on artificial intelligence [AI] and ethics, based on a series of hearings and research, designed to guide any future legislative debates on the subject. The study group created by the Lords included eminent sociologists as well as the Lord Bishop of Oxford.[73])

A reformed California senate could provide a template of sorts for just the kind of deliberative institution that can help reweave a new relationship between the *demos*, the public, and *res publica*, the institutions of public interest, in this new era in which political awakenings empowered by social media and a will to participate in direct democracy must be responsibly engaged.

Far from the old worry that such a senate would constitute an aristocracy, it would instead be a bulwark against the outsized power of the new plutocrats of avaricious digital capitalism, and of the already-established economic elites and organized special interests, which will continue seeking to use their immense resources to influence both electoral government and popular referenda and initiatives. It would also serve as a check on the immediate passions and prejudices of an unreflective public. In short, this "distinct" governmental body would help save democracy from itself, as the Founders intended.

California is certainly not yet ready to adopt the radical plan we propose. As in the early American states and in the states in the years before the Progressive Era, ideas need time to gestate and evolve, awaiting circumstances that make possible their realization. Given that direct democracy is more widely used in California than elsewhere, however, the experience we have outlined, as well as the reform solutions already undertaken and that we further propose, makes the state a laboratory for the third turn of democracy in much the same way Wisconsin was during the Progressive Era.

As *The Economist* wrote in 2011 in its report on the activities of the Think Long Committee and other public interest groups, "The next few years in California might see perhaps the liveliest debate about freedom and governance since the Federalists and Anti-Federalists argued in 1787–88 about whether or not to ratify America's new constitution. Lovers of democracy and liberty everywhere will study that old debate. Now they will also pay attention to California's, for it will provide lessons for everyone."[74]

CHAPTER 3

Redrawing the Social Contract

If machines produce everything we need, the
outcome will depend on how things are distributed.
Everyone can enjoy a life of luxurious leisure if the
machine-produced wealth is shared, or most people
can end up miserably poor if the machine-owners
successfully lobby against wealth redistribution. So
far, the trend seems to be toward the second option,
with technology driving ever-increasing inequality.

Stephen Hawking

If the dislocations of globalization have caused the economic insecurity that is driving populist discontent, the digital economy, as
the late Stephen Hawking noted, will be no less disruptive to the
work and livelihood of millions. The greatest immediate challenge democratic societies and their welfare states will have to
face, therefore, is dealing with the impact on labor displaced or
demoted by intelligent machines and the commensurate further
bifurcation of the workforce between high- and low-wage jobs.

Giving this oncoming reality, here is our key argument: The
paradox for governance in the age of digital capitalism is that the
more dynamic a perpetually innovating knowledge-driven economy, the more robust a redefined safety net and opportunity web

must be to cope with the steady disruption and gaps in wealth and power that will result. Mirroring the new distribution of social power in the information age, all must share in the wealth created by highly productive, but job-displacing or wage-depressing technologies. Today, Marx might put his famous dictum—"from each according to his abilities, to each according to his needs"—this way for the age of digital capitalism: from the digital economy's inability to provide work with a living wage, to each according to his or her needs.

Redrawing the social contract to reduce inequality in the digital age has two main clauses. First, a labor market more adaptable to the fluid shift of tasks in the workplace, cushioned by a universal net that protects the welfare of workers instead of specific jobs—a policy pioneered in the Scandinavian countries called *flexicurity.* Unemployment and health benefits must be provided universally by the state and not tied to a specific job or company.

Second, shifting focus from redistribution through taxation on wealth to *pre-distribution* policies that enhance the skills needed to navigate the steady disruptions of innovation and that bolster the capital assets of all citizens. Investment in public higher education to mend the main social fracture today—namely, the gap in education levels—is one key pillar of such a policy shift. The other is reducing inequality through a scheme in which all citizens own an equity share in the robots creating the new wealth of the future.

JOB LOSS AND INEQUALITY IN
THE DIGITAL AGE

Laura Tyson has been on top of every significant debate about the US economy for the past twenty-five years. As prosperity bloomed during the Bill Clinton era, she presided over the Council of Economic Advisers—its first-ever woman chair—and directed the White House National Economic Council. Now a professor at the University of California, Berkeley, Tyson has witnessed close-up the power of the digital revolution, from the dot-com boom of the 1990s through the recession that set in when the bubble burst, and into the accelerating change of the twenty-first century. Having seen the digital revolution catapult Google, Amazon, Facebook, and other internet startups into the ranks of the richest companies in the world, she does not doubt that it will deliver new waves of abundance as it further transforms the manufacturing and consumer economies.

But she believes such progress will likely come at the expense of ever fewer jobs and falling wages. Tyson's view is part of a growing consensus of thought leaders, from LinkedIn founder Reid Hoffman to entrepreneur-inventor Elon Musk, who worry what will happen to coming generations as the labor-displacing effect of digitization intensifies, creating vast wealth for the owners of technology and processors of big data while potentially shortchanging workers, both employed and unemployed. "There will be fewer and fewer jobs that a robot cannot do better," says Musk.[1]

As Professor Tyson put it in a paper coauthored with Nobel economist Michael Spence: "Technology is a major driver of productivity and economic growth—it creates prosperity. But the computer/digital revolution is also a major driver of inequality in a variety of ways: it favors more skilled over less skilled workers, it increases the return to capital owners over labor, it enables or 'turbo-charges' globalization by reducing employment and constraining wage growth for middle-income workers, particularly in manufacturing and tradeable services."[2]

How the benefits are shared and the pain of change is distributed will determine whether the digital future will be a fair or sustainable one.

"Who will own the robots?" is thus the seminal question, as Tyson posed it at *The WorldPost* "Future of Work" conference in London in February 2015. In these concerns she joins MIT economists Eric Brynjolfsson and Andrew McAfee, who foresee what they call a "Great Decoupling." For as long as those of us who grew up in modern America can remember, wages and jobs have risen in sync with economic productivity. But no more. Brynjolfsson and McAfee observe that wages as a share of GDP are today at an all-time low even as corporate profits soar; jobs and wages are being divorced from wealth creation. A generation ago, labor advocates worried about the offshoring of manufacturing jobs to low-wage nations. But now technological innovation overshadows globalization as the chief cause of growing inequality in the United States. As Brynjolfsson and McAfee put it, "Off-shoring is only a way-station on the way to automation."[3] According to a study from the Center for Business and Economic Research at Ball State University, when 5.6 million jobs disappeared between 2000 and 2010, productivity growth caused 85 percent of those job losses in manufacturing, while 13 percent were lost due to trade.[4]

The scope of the transformation is only now coming into view. It is vast: a study by the Oxford Martin School projects that fully 47 percent of US jobs are at risk from automation.[5] As the study notes, computerization historically has largely been confined to manual and cognitive routine tasks involving explicit rule-based activities. But with recent technological advances in artificial intelligence, user interfaces, and other fields, computerization is spreading to domains commonly defined as nonroutine, such as language translation and self-driving cars. According to the study, which examined 702 occupational categories, jobs at the highest risk of elimination include those in sales (cashiers, telemarketers, counter clerks) and services such as janitorial cleaning and construction in which automated prefabrication will take hold.[6] A 2018 study by the Organisation for Economic Co-operation and Development, which further breaks down tasks within categories—for example, differentiating between mechanics working on an assembly line and those working in neighborhood garages—estimates that 14 percent of jobs in the advanced economies would be subject to elimination through automation. It notes that the lowest-wage and -skilled jobs are most likely to be eliminated.[7] This likelihood is compounded by a growing gap between college-educated top-wage earners and those without skills at the bottom. In their paper, Tyson and Spence note that "during the past 30 years the real earnings gap between the median college-educated worker and the median high-school educated worker among US males working fulltime in year-round jobs has nearly doubled."[8]

If new wealth is not shared by the society at large, even as wages diminish and jobs are erased, the emergent knowledge-driven innovation economy that promises so much in other respects cannot endure. To address this challenge first requires understanding it—in particular, how the very idea of value is changing.

THE TRANSFORMATION OF CAPITAL BY KNOWLEDGE

While the "digital labor" of automation and robots is displacing real workers and white-collar employees who have mortgages to pay, families to feed, and children to educate, the nature of capital itself is also being transformed. These days, a clever algorithm conjured up by a college student who owns no other assets can morph into a billion-dollar company in a few short years. We have seen time and again that the biggest companies today—Alphabet/ Google, Facebook, Alibaba, TenCent—seem to emerge out of nowhere other than the fertile minds of visionary entrepreneurs. Already by 2015, Facebook, founded in 2004, had five times the market value of General Motors, founded in 1908.[9] GM produces automobiles with chassis, engines, and tires that must be assembled in large factories linked to a chain of parts suppliers and auto distributors. Facebook links you with like-minded friends and delivers news and information sympathetic to your worldview. Its algorithm is its means of production; your information is its product. At its height in the late 1970s, GM employed more than 600,000 people.[10] Facebook, still growing globally today, has more than 2 billion users—greater than the population of China—yet employs just over 30,000.[11]

Digital companies are ever more perfectly matching demand with supply, consumer with producer, in every realm from dating to divorce counseling to finding old car parts. Unlike brick-and-mortar enterprises, businesses built on information-processing software can reach vast scale virtually, by linking through the global network of the internet. The value that attracts market capitalization even before profits are earned is all that captured data about users. Big-data analysis enables sales targeting based on personal characteristics ranging from sexual orientation to consumer preference for one shampoo over another.

Labor and capital, brick and mortar, of course remain. But capturing a person's data is where the value lies. The ability to harvest that data coproduced by the consumer, as Google or Facebook does, is where large profits are made.[12]

As computing power continues to grow exponentially and "the cloud" offers infinite storage capacity, there seems no end to the possibilities. Blockchain technology offers a new way of storing and sharing data—including our personal records and finances. With big data and advanced analytics, all medical records can be searched for corresponding causes of disease. Entire genomes can readily and rapidly be mapped—and remixed. Just-in-time logistics will penetrate all industries, combining with three-dimensional manufacturing that eliminates the need for fore-casted inventory while decentralizing production and diminishing the demand for low-cost labor. The "internet of things," the ulti-mate convergence of the digital and physical, will bring untold new efficiencies once sensors are implanted in everything from tennis shoes to light switches to report back on personal use hab-its. Electric power grids across entire regions can be integrated to better allocate energy according to periods of peak and weak demand. Remote sensors on roads and in satellites, linked to sen-sors in cars, all connected in one mega–urban traffic grid, will manage the safe flow of self-driving vehicles. The McKinsey con-sulting firm projects that the enhanced productivity expected to result from this processed digitization could yield as much as $11 trillion a year in new wealth by 2025.[13]

It is this knowledge input or "digital capital," not the input of physical labor, and less and less the input of physical capital, that is the dominant driver of wealth creation in the twenty-first century.

Paradoxically, trying to understand these latest developments of hyperdynamic capitalism takes us back to one of its earliest critics—Karl Marx. His prescription of statist communism may well have proven among the most disastrous notions ever put into practice. But his analysis of the inner logic of capitalism remains in many ways unequaled and highly relevant today. Marx's central insight for his time was that labor was "the form-forging fire" that created value out of raw material. Indeed, that was the outstanding reality in front of his eyes as he observed the proletariat of his day breaking their backs in the "Satanic mills" of industrializing Europe. He made it the focus of his most famous work, *Das Kapital.* But Marx also foresaw that physical labor would not reign forever; as machines amplified human capacities, knowledge would one day replace it.

At his death, Marx left behind a major, unfinished manuscript entitled *Outline of the Critique of Political Economy* that was to have been his masterwork. It was wider-ranging than *Das Kapital,* and included among its eight hundred pages a seminal essay, "Fragments on the Machine," in which Marx grappled with the potential of technology and automation.[14] He saw clearly that "over time, the compulsion to cheapen commodities, and thereby maximize profit, by reducing labor costs causes the ratio of machines to workers in production to rise. It also concentrates wealth in proportionally ever-fewer hands and renders a great part of the population unemployed and, from the point of view of capital, superfluous."[15]

Marx was intrigued by the power of machines to amplify effort—that a locomotive operated by a single engineer could convey hundreds of tons of goods; that a lone telegraph operator could convey news across continents and oceans; that a "self-acting" cotton spinner, tended by 1 "minder" and 2 boys, could do the work of 1,320 women at spinning wheels. From these observations, the materialist philosopher drew a startling insight. Marx foresaw that knowledge and organization would ultimately displace labor as the key human inputs, changing the very nature of productivity and wealth creation.[16] He called this knowledge input "the general intellect."

Unlike labor or raw materials, knowledge is not scarce but abundant. It doesn't diminish like water or minerals as people consume it. It can be shared without ever being exhausted. Such characteristics turn the classical economics of Adam Smith, with its focus on the allocation of scarce resources, on its head. In Smith's view, the market defines value and maximizes efficiency through prices based on the meeting point of supply and demand. Yet the value of abundant knowledge is largely uncaptured in monetary prices or output per unit of production. This fact has large implications as the importance of shared knowledge grows. The expansion of value not measured by money complicates how wages, benefits, and contracts are negotiated and how poverty, wealth, and inequality are quantified. As digital technology diffuses throughout the economy, it is deflationary.

How the value of shared knowledge is captured—who owns the robots—thus becomes the central issue in the emergent hybrid political economy of the Internet Age. Slovenian philosopher Slavoj Žižek, a self-described postindustrial Marxist, has updated Marx's insight for today's knowledge economy, in which wealth accumulates out of all proportion to the physical labor put into creating it. In Žižek's modernized view, we are witnessing the gradual transformation of the profit generated by the "exploitation of labor" into "rent appropriated through the privatization of the general intellect." This, of course, is precisely what the business model of the giant social media companies is all about—making our personal data their proprietary product. When wealth accumulates because all of society has become a factory producing knowledge and exploitable data, Žižek believes, society will be forced to make a radical change. The profits will have to be shared more equitably with everyone.[17]

Further, conventional measurements of both gross domestic product (GDP) and productivity will have to be reassessed and recalibrated because they do not capture the intangible value-added activities of an economy driven by abundant knowledge instead of scarce inputs. As Erik Brynjolfsson noted in an interview, the inventor of the GDP metric, Simon Kuznets, made clear it measured not well-being but only economic output expressed in positive prices. Thus, as Brynjolfsson notes, if one lives ten years longer because of improved medical care, that is not measured in GDP. However, if one buys ten flat-screen TVs, GDP captures that.[18]

Tyson and Spence point to this new wrinkle in digital capitalism: "While digital capital intensive companies can and do generate high concentration of income and wealth, they also provide a range of digitally-based services that are widely available at very low cost." This means, they conclude, "that the distribution of 'benefits' from such services may be more equal than the distribution of wealth for the owners of the digital capital that provide such services."[19] The obvious case in point is the worldwide penetration of mobile internet connections, projected to reach 65 percent by 2020.

As cofounder of the X-Prize and Singularity University, Peter Diamandis, a hyperenergetic California entrepreneur-futurist, has a finger on the pulse of developments at the technological frontier. The X-Prize is a $10 million award given annually for innovations that "benefit mankind"; its judges include such high-tech luminaries as Elon Musk and Google cofounder Larry Page. With AI enthusiast Ray Kurzweil, Diamandis set up Singularity University at the NASA Research Park in Silicon

Valley to focus on the world-changing possibilities of convergent technologies.

Diamandis believes that the distributed nature of digital capitalism is profoundly transforming all the familiar production and consumption patterns of the past. During the industrial revolution of the late nineteenth century, he argues, "production was basically a one-for-one proposition. If a capitalist wanted to double output, he or she had to double the number of factory workers or the amount of machines. In the digital age, the marginal cost of replicating data is near zero and the marginal cost of distribution is near zero. You can produce and distribute an app, a document, or a service a million-fold or a billion-fold at almost no new incremental cost."[20] Indeed, the scope of markets has expanded to breathtaking scale. *Time* Magazine listed Snapchat as its most popular app of 2016, with 158 million daily active users.[21] "So today," Diamandis continues, "any single individual or start-up entrepreneur can impact the lives of millions or billions of people without the huge costs of capital, as used to be the case."

This process is disruptive, needless to say, because any innovation that creates a new market disrupts an old one. "We have seen how digital pixels replaced Kodak analog film cameras that needed photographic chemicals and paper," says Diamandis. He adds that at its height, Kodak had "144,000 employees and a $10 billion market capitalization." Instagram reached that same market cap with "only 13 employees." What follows from this, Diamandis contends, is

> demonetization, dematerialization and democratization. Those digital pictures cost nothing—demonetization—to take or transmit once you've got a smartphone. The smartphone is also a prime example of dematerialization—its functions concentrate in one small device the capabilities of old IBM machines that filled whole

rooms, landline phones, cameras and watches. When cost falls so dramatically with dematerialization, you get democratization—smartphones are affordable to billions of people empowered now as never before with devices that were once only available to a few. Democratization is the logical result of demonetization and dematerialization.[22]

Not surprisingly, conventional measures of productivity based on output per labor and capital input fail to capture the nature of these profound shifts. What no doubt accounts for the drop in productivity is in part the exhaustion of gains from industrial-era inventions and in part the decades it takes for the diffusion of technology throughout the entire economy to register an impact.

But it is surely also a result of the massive expansion of low-wage and low-productivity services (from personal care workers to teachers and sales clerks) that now dominate employment in the nontradeable and tech-dominated sectors of advanced economies. As Michael Spence showed in his 2012 book, *The Next Convergence,* 90 percent of the 27 million jobs created in the two decades previous to his study were in the nontradeable sector, such as retail, health care, and government services.[23]

The creation of fewer high-paying skilled jobs among those exposed to competition in the globalized tradeable economy, the elimination of middle-level routine work by automation in both factories and offices, and the expansion of employment in low-wage services that cannot be outsourced or automated have polarized the labor market. As Spence notes, "the tradeable sector is roughly 35–40 percent of the total economy in the US and other developed countries, somewhat less in employment terms. The nontradeable sector is very large, accounting for roughly 2/3 of value added. Its share of employment is even larger, currently over 70 percent and climbing steadily toward 80 percent."[24]

This reality drags the overall conventional measurements down. By definition, high-tech, high-productivity sectors will shrink employment relative to output, but low-productivity services will account for most new jobs. Clearly, a new bifurcation is accelerating between this sector and the highly productive and highly profitable knowledge-driven technology sector with broad exposure to the global economy. In short, the employment is not where the productivity is, and productivity and is not where the employment is. How to articulate this bifurcated economy in order to cope with the rising challenge of inequality while rewarding value and sharing wealth across these sectors should be at the top of any reform agenda.

THE PARALLEL SHARING ECONOMY

As innovation in the digital world converges with the physical economy through exponential technologies, from 3-D manufacturing to sensor-efficient renewable energy and transportation, all connected through "the internet of things," we are entering what futurist Jeremy Rifkin calls the "third industrial revolution."[25] (Others call it the "fourth industrial revolution," separating digital innovations from their integration with things.) Because demonetization and democratization diffuse wealth and power at near-zero marginal cost, Rifkin envisions a post-capitalist sharing economy that grows up alongside the profit-driven capitalism of the likes of Uber and Air B&B. This culture, says Rifkin, is already taking hold and has the potential to mitigate the worst problems of economic insecurity cited by

Laura Tyson and others (see the outset of this chapter). Whether that mitigation suffices depends on the extent to which the sharing economy can provide a living income, to be supplemented (as discussed below) by broad participation in the equity growth of the for-profit economy or by other measures to boost income.

As the sharing economy grows, conventional ownership may yield in many arenas to access on demand, such as shared pools of self-driving cars that can be accessed as easily as downloaded music and software today. If the attitudes of millennials today are any guide, a kind of "quantum economy" is on track to develop in many areas. The value of money will diminish with respect to those assets since access to them will be comparatively cheap. Visionaries like Tesla's Elon Musk even expect nominal wages, despite their low level, to rise in real value as digital efficiencies drive down prices.

"Prosumers"—consumers who produce their own goods and services—are bound to disintermediate many activities formerly delivered through the market and do it themselves, manufacturing their own shoes at home or at a special shop using 3D printing, for example, instead of buying shoes at Walmart or ordering from Zappos. Big-box discounters and Amazon may well be only way stations to "prosumption," as the futurist Alvin Toffler envisioned in his last book.[26] Homeowners who have installed a solar energy source not only produce their own energy already but generate capacity to sell back to the grid. In an age of climate change an ethos of sharing over singular ownership makes more efficient use of resources. Its flexible nature will enable more freedom and broader experiences. It is more affordable.

As the decades-long transition to this twenty-first century political economy unfolds, there will be big bumps along the road for the safety net and other policies to address.

THE FUTURE OF WORK

While the digital revolution will eventually displace many jobs, building the infrastructure to support leaps in productivity will, as we have seen, create jobs in the intermediate term—provided that the financial system and public policy are properly aligned. From high-speed rail, to two-way energy grids, to networks of recharging stations for electric cars and trucks, to installing sensors and retrofitting homes and workplaces, the demand for job-intensive infrastructure modernization is deep and widespread globally. At least in the intermediate term, the experience of Amazon shows that the logistical efficiency of robots can lead to more demand and thus the growth of business that adds more jobs. In 2017 Amazon indeed added 100,000 jobs in response to increased demand.[27] Longtime Cisco chief John Chambers estimates that digitizing the European economy alone can create 850,000 jobs.[28] Mo Ibrahim, the African mobile-phone pioneer and Celtel magnate, has demonstrated that the spread of cellular technology in Africa has created a wave of new jobs. "By 2004, Celtel was operating in 13 African countries," he told us at a Paris conclave of the Berggruen Institute in 2014. In a follow-up interview, Ibrahim told us that "besides our direct employment, we had 340,000 entrepreneurs who set up small shops to sell scratch cards and thousands of others working on contracts for maintenance of our towers and reselling our electrical generators and batteries—maybe 400,000 altogether. Taking into account we were operating in only 13 countries and there were other operators in our market, I suspect we are talking about 3 or 4 million people employed because of new cell phone technology."[29] Of the 800 million inhabitants of sub-Saharan Africa, 80 percent are projected to have cellphones by 2020, many of whom never had land lines, leading some to assign to Africa the moniker "the mobile continent."[30] For Africa as a whole, there were 557 million unique mobile subscribers in 2016, making it the world's second-largest market, but also still the least penetrated.[31]

What is true for Europe and sub-Saharan Africa is also true for other continents and regions. Building out the foundations of the third industrial revolution in the United States and elsewhere can create massive employment instead of job displacement—if the proper public policies, including apprenticeship training programs and investment in education and infrastructure are put in place. This is a big *if*. Here too, governance will determine outcomes.

The Precariat

Arguably the most important new socioeconomic class to emerge with the advent of the twenty-first-century political economy is the so-called precariat—ex-middle-class workers and young people just entering the workforce who struggle to get by in low-paying, insecure jobs, often without benefits.

The Aspen Institute has estimated that as much as 22 percent of the American workforce is already employed in this "gig" economy, characterized by freelance work.[32] Reforms aimed at improving competitiveness in the global economy and opening labor markets to create new jobs have introduced flexible hours and part-time work across the Western democracies—likely the standard for the future. Secure lifetime employment in one job, or even one occupation, is likely a relic of the past.

For former US secretary of labor Robert Reich, the bally-hooed arrival of sharing economy companies like Uber are a labor nightmare come true. He calls them the logical culmination of a process that began thirty years ago when corporations began turning over full-time jobs to temporary workers, independent contractors, free-lancers, and consultants. It was a way to shift risks and uncertainties onto the workers—work that might entail more hours than planned for, or was more stressful than expected. And a way to circumvent labor laws that set minimal standards for wages, hours, and working conditions. And that enabled employees to join together to bargain for better pay and benefits. The new on-demand work shifts risks entirely onto workers, and eliminates minimal standards completely.[33]

Reich is primarily addressing the United States, where the labor market is among the most flexible—and least secure—in the advanced world and where the so-called gig economy has spread rapidly. The effort to adjust in Europe, where strong labor movements in the past century codified into law job security and generous benefits, reveals better than anywhere else the trade-offs between the old economy and the disruptive new one. Yet adjust Europe must, not only to be in a globally competitive position to afford some future semblance of its present welfare state, but also to create employment for young people. Youth unemployment remains the premier challenge in Greece, Spain, and Italy.[34]

The ability to improve competitiveness in the global economy and enhance productivity is imperative if Europe is to sustain its social model and get out from under the burden of debt it has incurred financing it. German chancellor Angela Merkel has pointedly said, "If Europe today accounts for just over 7 percent of the world's population, produces around 25 percent of global GDP and has to finance 50 percent of global social spending, then it's obvious that it will have to work very hard to maintain its prosperity and way of life."[35] In the face of high unemployment and weak economic growth in Germany in 2005, then-chancellor Gerhard Schroeder initiated a series of labor market and welfare reforms to reboot a stalling economy. Among other changes, those reforms cut unemployment benefits from thirty-two to no more than twenty-four months. They also allowed employers to offer workers fixed six-month contracts—so-called minijobs—instead of committing to long-term employment with the full social benefits that were the foundation of the social market policies of the industrial era.

Germany has since recovered its competitiveness to the point that its trade surplus has swelled year upon year.[36] When the 2008–9 financial crisis struck, German companies were able to cut output by laying off temporary workers while retaining a skilled core workforce for use when the economy turned up. A negative consequence, however, appeared years after Schroeder's reforms were implemented: growing inequality between high-skilled workers whose jobs remain protected and lower-skilled and lower-wage temporary workers. Of all EU countries, Germany has the highest proportion of low-wage employees, about 20 percent of the workforce between ages twenty-five and thirty-four. In an attempt to limit inequality, Germany in 2015 instituted an hourly minimum wage of 8.50 Euros[37] (which it raised again in 2017, to 8.84 Euros[38]).

Spain and other countries struggling to escape Europe's prolonged slowdown have adopted minijob reforms of their own, with similarly mixed results: greater economic resilience but more precarious employment and greater inequality.[39] In France, Emmanuel Macron, the pro-business president of France elected in 2017, has pushed through reforms that open the labor market while encouraging a new "start-up" economic environment that undoes the dirigiste model of the past. The stance of French unions will make all the difference in France. As the Nordic countries have shown in practice, strengthening instead of weakening unions is a key to improving equality—but only if the unions don't resist innovation, but assist it and use their bargaining power to gain a greater share of the wealth created by productivity gains. Part and parcel of the social bargain Macron is promising is, Nordic style, to enlarge the safety net and expand training programs in tandem with more flexibility in hiring and firing, both of which will surely become more intense the deeper France treads into the perpetually disruptive digital innovation economy. To achieve both objectives, France, like all other nations, will need a tax system that reaps enough fiscal benefits from a more flexible economy to pay for a net that will catch the increasing number of workers who fall into the gaps opened by the creative-destructive churn of wealth creation.

The new jobs of the gig economy cause their own kinds of social tension as well, reflecting both national character and economic circumstance. In socially protectionist France in January 2016, strikes against Uber by licensed taxi drivers gridlocked Paris. Yet, at the same time, for Senegalese immigrant youth in the banlieux, the impoverished high-rise suburbs that ring Paris, Uber offered opportunity. They started their own companies as Uber drivers because it was the only work to be found.[40]

Meanwhile, in upwardly mobile Estonia, where per capita annual income has risen from $1,000 in the immediate post-Soviet era to $20,000 today, President Toomas Hendrik Ilves, who left office in 2016, welcomed the ride-sharing service. He saw it as a potent way to turn car owners into capitalists, matching demand for transportation by people who don't own cars with supply from drivers who do.[41]

Time for a New Social Contract

What is certain is that the impact of technological advance is so great that it will force a rethinking of our political and social institutions in ways no less profound than the introduction of the welfare state by Otto von Bismarck in nineteenth-century Prussia and the New Deal of Franklin Roosevelt in the 1930s United States.[42]

We contend that the role of governance is not to resist the inevitable but to smooth the transition between the past and the future by balancing the benefits of innovation against the negatives of disruption—a process that requires a renovation of governance. Its daunting challenge is to maintain social stability and promote inclusiveness even as economic turbulence becomes a permanent fact of life.

To cope with continuous disruption, the social safety nets of the Industrial Age must be reconceived both to accommodate the constant flux of rapid technological development and trade competition in the structure of industry, and to protect the overall welfare of workers instead of specific jobs. That means universal unemployment and retraining benefits, as well as health coverage not linked to a given employer. This model, which already exists in some Scandinavian countries and is being promoted elsewhere in Europe, is called *flexicurity*. Further, in a knowledge-driven innovation economy, the old idea of a net must morph into an "opportunity web" that offers the preparation needed to ensure access to high-skilled jobs that robots won't displace. The social support system must become more than a net cushioning against a temporary fall—the loss of a job. It must also serve as a trampoline for boosting chances.

Governance must also address the gaps in wealth and power that will result as rapid technological advance displaces labor, diminishes labor's role relative to capital, and divorces productivity and wealth creation from employment. This means ensuring that all citizens can attain a livable income. A parallel can be drawn between our current period and what historian Robert Allen has called "Engel's Pause."[43] It was out of the period when the disruptions of the first industrial revolution outweighed its future benefits that the welfare state was born. Similarly, today, a new social contract needs to emerge that addresses our own era of technological advance and turmoil. And it will do so, as always in history, only if social forces are mobilized around a cogent political program that demands it.

Remedies can be delivered in several forms. But to be effective, any systemic response must enable the public to share in the new wealth that the digital revolution is creating.

In his highly influential *Capital in the Twenty-First Century*, Thomas Piketty rightly identifies the source of economic inequality as the differential between the awesome earning power of those who possess capital and the unrewarding slog of wageworkers.[44] Those with money to invest can reap compounding returns; those who labor can expect, at best, to earn what the market is willing to pay. Piketty argues forcefully that progressive taxation—not only of income but also of wealth—is the way to right the imbalance.

As wealth concentrates more and more in the top percentiles associated with the large digital monopolies and financial corporations, Piketty is right, as far as he goes. But he ventures only halfway toward a real solution. In fact, the rest of the key to reducing inequality is turning Thomas Piketty's analysis on its head—by focusing not solely on redistributing income but also on sharing the wealth of returns on investment. To avoid a society in which most citizens' economic circumstances are determined only by their meager earnings as Uber drivers,

Airbnb hosts, or elderly-care assistants, instead of by incomes from lifelong careers, everyone must own an investor's stake in the wealth and productivity that innovations generate. Equity sharing is the best way to level the playing field. Notes British economist Anthony Atkinson, "Debate about wealth tends to focus on large fortunes at the top, but the redistribution of wealth is as much about the encouragement of small savings at the bottom as it is about restriction of excesses at the top."[45]

Reducing inequality in the age of digital capitalism must go beyond the old idea of redistribution carried out by a distrusted state and instead focus on enhancing endowments both in education and capital ownership across the population. Economist Branko Milanovic has put it succinctly: "The only promising avenue to reduce inequality are interventions that are undertaken before taxes and transfers kick in. These include a reduction in the inequality of endowments, especially inequality in education and the ownership of assets. If market income inequality can be controlled, and over time curbed, government redistribution via transfers and taxes can also become much less important."[46]

Taking the transformation of capitalism we have described into account, several features would constitute the basis of a new social contract. In combination and over time, these features would meet the dual challenge of reducing inequality and creating social security amid the steady disruptions of the innovation economy. Some of the features are realizable in the near future; others will require a longer-term evolution from the status quo.

FLEXICURITY AND PRE-DISTRIBUTION

The central feature of a new social contract for the digital age is the combination of *flexicurity* and *pre-distribution*. This article of the new social contract entails, as discussed earlier, the design of flexible labor market policies that protect workers instead of jobs in an ever-shifting innovation economy, including universal benefits and training; investment in public higher education to close the income gap between high- and low-wage opportunities; and an equity share for all in the wealth generated by digital capitalism, wealth creation that is itself fueled by the data generated by users and consumers. Ultimately, one can envision the ownership of all large enterprises being apportioned among three categories of shareholder—private investors, employees, and the public at large.

Piketty has convincingly shown that progressive taxation reduces inequality—which indeed was at its lowest point in the United States in the years between the end of World War II and 1980, when the top marginal income tax rate was 81 percent. Yet this was also the period of highest productivity growth, as industrial manufacturing matured and its multiplier effects rippled through the American economy. But that is only part of the story.[47]

Unremarked in Piketty's analysis is the fact that the period he applauds was precisely the era when vast public investment in education and infrastructure during prior decades had its mature impact. The great public universities, such as the California State University system with its twenty-three campuses and 470,000 students, were fully built out after World War II, as was the interstate highway system that connects the East and West Coasts. These complemented the great public works projects of the 1930s, such as Hoover Dam and the Tennessee Valley Authority. Such public investments, combined with rising wages due to productivity leaps in the manufacturing economy, propelled the rise of the American middle class.

Certainly, there remains a case for progressive taxation to limit the gap between the top 1 percent and the rest. But public investment is the necessary other half of the equation. Ed Kleinbard, a University of Southern California economist who for years was chief of staff of the Joint Committee on Taxation of the US Congress, has argued for an approach aimed at the *overall progressive outcome* of tax policy. He argues that even if taxes now are less progressive than at the height of the United States' generalized prosperity, or even if they're regressive, what matters more is how government revenues are spent. For Kleinbard, investment in public higher education and infrastructure, including digital networks, is the key to upward mobility. It is the less well off, he says, who use education benefits to maximum advantage. Indeed, a Stanford University study of all American universities in 2017 showed that California State University Los Angeles was the top school in the nation in fostering upward mobility. More of its students from the bottom 20 percent of income cohort made it to the top 20 percent in the years after graduation than at any other institution surveyed.[48] And infrastructure investment creates well-paying jobs for the working class.[49] Spending on both infrastructure and higher education disproportionately benefits the less well off.

On the basis of extensive modeling of the California economy and its tax base, and following Kleinbard's idea, our Think Long Committee has proposed a comprehensive overhaul of the present tax system. As we touch upon in the previous chapter, California's $2.6 trillion economy has shifted from one based mainly on agriculture and manufacturing in the 1950s and 1960s, when the framework of today's fiscal structure was set up, to one based on information and services, the two sectors that now account for 80 percent of all economic activities in the state. Yet the service economy in California is barely taxed except for a few odd services like welding. It is only common sense that the tax system should reflect the real economy of the twenty-first century while retaining its signature progressive character. Levying a small consumption tax on the broad base of the service economy, with a commensurate income tax cut for the middle class and small businesses, would raise the necessary revenues for investment in public higher education and infrastructure.

This plan also better suits a state that is undergoing dramatic demographic change. The youthful Latino and Asian populations that will largely constitute California's future electorate are seeking to *build their assets* through upward mobility. For aspirational constituencies striving to reach the middle class, opportunity to rise on the foundation of public investment is paramount.

AN EQUITY SHARE FOR ALL CITIZENS: UNIVERSAL BASIC CAPITAL

As labor-displacing and wage-depressing technologies and the sharing economy grow in the coming decades, it is imperative to prepare postwelfare institutions that can provide a *dividend for all citizens,* enabling them to share in the new wealth even as employment is increasingly divorced from productivity. This can be done in several, overlapping ways.

The most readily adaptable model for an equity-sharing plan in an advanced economy like that of the United States would involve a mandatory national savings and investment fund. A few nations, such as Singapore and Australia, have such funds already. Participation would be mandatory for all working adults and would require employer, employee, and government contributions. Australia's Superannuated Fund explains itself to its members thus: "During your working life you make contributions to your super fund and the earnings you receive are reinvested, building up the value over time. The money that you put into your super fund must generally stay there until you reach retirement, or when you begin your transition to retirement, both after a set minimum age. As contributions to your super fund and their earnings are generally taxed at just 15%, this makes it one of the most tax-effective investment vehicles."[50] The California legislature passed a bill in 2016 along these lines to create the California Secure Choice Retirement Plan, which established a state investment fund available to all citizens whose employer does not offer a private plan. In this scheme, companies with five employees or more are required to put aside 2–5 percent of monthly wages into 401(k) plans unless workers opt out. Illinois, Oregon, and Connecticut are considering similar plans.[51]

While the returns on investment through the Australian fund reduce inequality by boosting the assets of smaller savers, it is limited to retirement. Singapore's Central Provident Fund (CPF) is a bit closer to what we have in mind in that, after a designated vesting period, the fund can be drawn upon for health and housing needs, not just retirement. Employer and employee contributions to the fund are mandatory up to the vesting minimum.[52]

In his book *Inequality: What Is to Be Done?* British economist Anthony Atkinson suggests such a fund be invested across a diversified portfolio of the market, like an indexed mutual fund, so returns reflect the growth of the entire economy.[53] In his plan, the fund would have a guaranteed, inflation-adjusted minimum rate of return determined by the historical average of a composite index over time. It could rise depending on the market, but could not fall below a designated floor, and would be subsidized, if necessary, in any given year by government financing. A reasonable portion of such a fund could be allocated to venture capital—giving the public equity in the upside of high-risk but potentially high-growth startups.[54] Both funds would be independently and professionally managed.

At present, 60 percent of American households have no mutual fund or 401(k) investments. And, of course, almost by definition, the 40-some percent that do own such funds are at the top end of the income scale, are employed in the tradeable or hi-tech sectors of the economy, and are less likely to be displaced by technology.[55] According to the Federal Reserve, 40 percent of adults in the United States don't have $400 to spare even as an emergency expense.[56]

Conceivably, everyone could participate in a "citizen's account" to which the earnings would accrue. Such an account would be mobile and travel with the member wherever he or she lives and works as the member negotiates the ever-more-flexible labor market.

While agreeing that such a fund makes sense, former US treasury secretary Lawrence Summers notes the conundrum it poses for a country like the United States: "The way you establish funds like that is to build chronic budget surpluses—not something the US is likely to see for a long while." Bill Gates's idea of a robot tax could be an important policy to start with now in order to build up the assets of these sovereign wealth funds so they can invest for the public at large, to whom they can then distribute the dividends. But, as Larry Summers also points out, such a tax makes sense only as a transitional measure because it would be counterproductive to impede the wealth creation you are trying to share.[57]

Eric Schmidt, who spent years as the top executive at Google, has drawn a parallel between digital capital and natural resources. How a nation manages this new "resource" of the twenty-first century, he argues, will determine its future prosperity. He compares how well Norway has fared managing the returns on state-owned energy resources versus Venezuela's squandering of its main petroleum assets.[58] In this sense, what we are proposing for the new digital resource is similar to what Norway has already done with its oil. Norway's sovereign wealth pool known as Government Pension Fund Global, financed by oil revenues, pays out dividends from fund investments to the public via pensions.[59]

The idea of sharing in the digital economy has so far come from companies like Airbnb, Uber, and Lyft and has been controlled by venture capital–backed private corporations. But digital innovations themselves promise another alternative, by providing a technological mechanism that enables sharing. At its core, the technology of blockchain is a mechanism for securely keeping track of information—for example, about ownership and transactions. Rather than storing the information in a central location, blockchain makes multiple copies and distributes them across all the nodes of a network. Nothing is held centrally. Each transaction is propagated across the network at essentially zero cost and with total transparency.

This capacity has profound implications for enabling an authentic sharing economy for all instead of just venture capitalists and traditional shareholders. For example, each new robot in an autonomous vehicle fleet could be fractionally owned by every member of the community in which it operates. Every time someone purchases a ride in one of the vehicles, rather than the income going only to a private company, it could be distributed to everyone in the community. Similarly, blockchain could be a mechanism whereby large social media companies such as Facebook and Google that profit enormously from using our personal information could pay us our fair share for the use of that data. This capability makes blockchain a potentially powerful accelerant for ensuring that everyone can own a share of the wealth—a form of social ownership that is not socialism, because it does not go through the state. It is a nonstate and non-bureaucratic form of distributing wealth.

This approach, combined with other predistribution policies such as public investment in higher education, on-the-job vocational training, and infrastructure, would address inequality at its root by enhancing ownership of assets across a broad public. Instead of waiting for inequality to happen and then addressing it via redistributive taxation or a universal basic income, it makes more sense to provide universal basic capital. Using blockchain to enable such a distributed, democratic ownership structure could give everyone a stake in our roboticized future, instead of deepening inequality.

There may be many paths to get from here to there. But the frame is clear: the best way to reduce inequality in the age of digital capitalism that diminishes income from labor is for all to have an equity share in new wealth creation.

UNIVERSAL BASIC INCOME AS A FLOOR

A related idea gaining attention is a "universal basic income" for every citizen whether he or she can find work or not. "With automation, there will come abundance," Elon Musk has said. "Almost everything will get very cheap."[60] For that reason, he envisions the inevitability, and affordability, of a universal basic income.

Such a scheme could be integrated into the universal investment fund outlined above, with the "basic income" serving as the guaranteed floor, to be supplemented by income from "basic capital" investment returns. Relying on a guaranteed income alone is a stretch because of the immense cost. When the Swiss voted down a referendum that would have instituted universal basic income at \$1,600 per person, it was estimated that it would cost a whopping 30 percent of GDP. The tax burden required to support that would evidently be self-defeating.[61]

In more modest schemes, a "participation income" or "conditional basic income" would be paid only to those who contribute to society in ways other than market labor through spans of universal public service, whether neighborhood safety, environmental cleanup, military service, or continuing education to upgrade skills. The idea of a society providing basic income must also imply social obligations.

Still others have proposed government wage-subsidy vouchers that would reduce the costs to employers of hiring low-wage workers, especially for socially beneficiary jobs, such as elderly care, in industries in which companies operate as nonprofits or on slim margins. This alternative to minimum-wage regulations would also provide a floor supplemented by the income from universal basic capital.

Other, hybrid ideas are circulating today as well. Carlos Slim, among the world's richest persons and a disciple of "Third Wave" futurist Alvin Toffler, advocates a three-day workweek combined with a limited guaranteed basic income.[62] Such a practice would spread available employment among more people as technology displaces jobs. This notion comes close to John Maynard Keynes's expectation in his 1930 essay "Economic

Possibilities for Our Grandchildren" that the wealth of industrialized nations would enable them to one day institute a fifteen-hour workweek.[63]

A POSTCAPITALIST SCENARIO

Ultimately, one can imagine a postcapitalist scenario that would involve completely overhauling corporate ownership. Suppose every sizable company in the economy were required to parcel its equity into thirds—one-third to belong to private investors, one-third to be owned by the employees, and one-third be owned by the public at large in the kind of universal investment funds we have proposed. This public stake would not only create an equity share for all but also bridge the chasm between investors and employees that, as Piketty has pointed out, is the root cause of inequality.

Far-fetched as this idea may seem, already hundreds of companies in the United States today are at least 50 percent owned by their employees. Other aspects of this vision are now a reality in many parts of the world. To take but one example, the German state of Lower Saxony owns a 20 percent stake in Volkswagen.[64]

The question we pose at the outset of this chapter is, "Who owns the robots?" The answer would be "We all do" if some combination of the schemes we have outlined could be realized. Only such an inclusive sharing of the new wealth generated by the innovation economy can make it socially sustainable. Such a scheme answers the economic anxiety which has fueled populist movements that blame their travails on immigrants or global trading partners. The moment may not yet have arrived for a consensus on this view, but it will come sooner or later because there is no alternative. Shared ownership is the only viable "nonzero" solution—the only solution that fairly benefits all—to the challenges posed by the new economy of digitally transformed capitalism.

CHAPTER 4

Harnessing Globalization

Globalization 1.0 was born out of the American-led world order that succeeded in rebuilding stability and prosperity in the core nations of the West and Japan after World War II. In the wake of the end of the Cold War, the so-called Washington Consensus of free trade, liberalized capital flows, deregulation, and integration of markets spread prosperity further, if unevenly, to a growing middle class in the emerging economies of South Korea, China, India, Brazil, and elsewhere. These developments have in turn led to Globalization 2.0, in which the drivers of globalization are increasingly outside the Western core economies.

Guiding the project of globalization may no longer be the sole province of its progenitors, but its infrastructure and momentum remain. Globalization is here to stay, albeit with the shoe now on the other foot. Harnessing its benefits while containing its damaging aspects when others are in the driver's seat is the new challenge ahead for the United States and the rest of the West.

If the most profound development of the latter half of the twentieth century and the early twenty-first century has been globalization, its most pronounced aspect has been the ascent of China from impoverishment to the top ranks of the globalized economy. The introduction of hundreds of millions of low-wage workers into an integrated global labor and open-trading market transformed China into the factory of the world, contributing—along with, or in conjunction with, technological advance—to the decimation of manufacturing across vast swaths of the West and the livelihood of whole communities that depended on it. Among those in the West who live in the rust belts left behind and who have fueled present-day populism, globalization is a scourge synonymous with China.

China's economic rise has also meant the most significant challenge to American dominance of the geopolitical order since the end of the Cold War.

In short, if the West wants to harness globalization so that it works for the average person, it has no choice but to do so either in conflict or in cooperation with China. For better or worse, the Middle Kingdom has returned to the center of the world stage. What it does, or doesn't, do, whether battling climate change, engaging in trade wars, or conquering the latest technologies, will affect all others. To understand China is to familiarize ourselves with our future.

THE CHINA CHALLENGE

"China won't be a democracy and it won't be an honorary member of the West."
Lee Kuan Yew

China's rise is helping to drive democratic renovation in the West precisely because it challenges the United States and others to move beyond the post–Cold War complacency in which liberal democracy was seen to have triumphed once and for all over other forms of governance. To peg China as a successor to the moribund Soviet Union and thus bound to fail in the future is to draw on the power of the wrong metaphor. China's resilience has much more to do with the millennia-long history of its institutional civilization than with the few decades of the disastrous social experiment of Maoism. To get a handle on the challenge—and to humbly assess what we might absorb from China's experience, instead of rejecting it outright—means understanding how the Chinese system actually works. We've found that even the most prominent strategic minds who have dealt with China, dating back to Nixon's opening in 1971, know little about the actual internal operations of the Communist Party and its governing mindset—which is itself further evolving as the personalist rule of Xi Jinping takes hold. To learn more, we have been going to Beijing since 2013 to meet the country's top leaders in an effort to better understand the modern Middle Kingdom.

Meeting the Red Emperor

It is an eerie feeling to whiz along vast highways devoid of traffic as far as the eye can see at the very heart of one of the world's largest megacities. That is what we experienced as our motorcade made its way through Beijing to the Great Hall of the People on Tiananmen Square, where we were scheduled to meet with President Xi Jinping. Along the entire seventy-kilometer route from our lodgings at Yanqui Lake on the outskirts of the city, the roads had been cleared of all vehicles in both directions. All feeder roads and on-ramps were blocked, leading to enormous traffic jams. We were witnessing firsthand the sharp contrast between the scope of authority in East and West. This, we thought, is what the encompassing power of China's Communist Party rulers looks and feels like.

If the center of gravity of the world order is shifting eastward, understanding China is key to understanding the future. To gauge that path ahead, the Berggruen Institute's 21st Century Council—which includes several Nobel laureates, sixteen former heads of state, and tech titans from Google, Twitter, Snapchat, LinkedIn, and Alibaba, among others—has in the past few years sponsored regular meetings with Xi and other top leaders.[1]

What interests us most about China is also the most difficult for Westerners to grasp: its form of consensual, instead of adversarial, governance. Going back three thousand years to the Zhou Dynasty—which lasted longer than the entire existence of the United States—the concept of "the political" in Chinese philosophy has meant minimizing conflict through reconciling different interests, rather than the more Western notion of us-versus-them contestation. This was known as the *tianxia* system, according to which "all under heaven" coexisted in harmony. Unlike the "external pluralism" of multiple competing parties and autonomous civil society in the West, the modern Chinese system has been characterized by "internal pluralism," in which a wide range of interests are represented, contend with one another, and are absorbed under the big tent of the 90 million–member Communist Party. Though composed of diverse currents of thought and orientation, Party processes and procedures reconcile differences to forge singular policies.

Thus, instead of dividing the body politic against itself as in Western multiparty systems, China's one-party system and the related institutions that codify policy into law—namely, the National People's Congress and the National People's Consultative Conference (which include the likes of basketball star Yao

Ming and Jackie Chan)—are designed to reach consensus regarding long-term goals that then have the decisive thrust to be carried out over the course of many years without a break in continuity. Although rough-and-tumble political disputes occur and sometimes even break out in the open, once consensus is forged internally, the policy path is followed with relative discipline by a leadership and administration that are largely meritocratic, if too often menaced by corruption, and are not based on popular appeal to an electorate.

China's leaders regard this system as better for the society as a whole than Western democracy and, above all, more inclusive and stable. Wang Huning, the top Communist Party theorist, argues that electoral democracy is a kind of sham. He has compared it to stockholders in a corporation in which everyone who owns a share theoretically has a voice, but in reality the company is controlled by those with the largest minority share. For Wang, intraparty democracy, in which there is competition over policies, is a superior way to make sure plural voices are heard. That also suits China's traditional cultural context in which meritocratic competition among officials has played the same central role in governance as popular elections have in the West. Trying to graft the Western system onto China would be a mistake, certainly for the foreseeable future, since, in Wang's view, it would "overstep the country's developmental level." Wang uses a Chinese proverb to make his point: "You can't help a seedling grow taller by pulling it out of its soil."[2]

As hard as it may be for the West to grasp, it is equally important to note in this respect that China's leaders today take Marxist ideology seriously. They believe in what they consider the scientific laws of development of productive forces—namely, that the market is necessary to create sufficient prosperity for the wealth thus generated to be shared in the next stage of socialism. According to the materialist roadmap, social relations—and political reforms—follow "the developmental level" along this road. In their minds, this "Sinicized Marxism" justifies the present transitional stage in which a fiercely competitive marketplace exists alongside state-owned enterprises that dominate the economy—the so-called socialist market economy with Chinese characteristics. As long ago as 1988, Hu Qili, then the Party's ideology chief and the youngest member of the Standing Committee of the Politburo, told one of the authors: "The market is not a feature unique to capitalism. Capitalism does not have the patent right over the market economy. What we are trying to create is a modality where the state regulates the market and the market guides the enterprises."[3]

In China all top leaders must pass through the Central Party School, where this worldview is inculcated. Very few get near the top unless they have proven themselves through long experience in governing provinces the size of large European nations. Xi Jinping's road to power, for example, stretched from serving as head of a production unit in a small town in Shaanxi province to being party secretary and governor of Fujian (37 million population) and Zhejiang (48 million population) provinces before ascending to the Party Standing Committee and later to the Politburo, then to the top post as president and Party secretary.[4]

It is these core attributes that have enabled the country to raise 700 million people—a population roughly double the size of the United States'—out of poverty in only thirty years, not to speak of other striking accomplishments such as building a vast network of high-speed rail lines along with other infrastructure to modernize a backward country in record time. One need only compare the progress over the past few decades in China with that in India, which has a Western-style democratic adversarial system, to see the merits of this alternative system of governance. Fifty percent of households in India don't have access to toilets seventy years after its independence from British rule.[5]

The chief flaw of China's system, of course, is closely linked to it strength: to prevent the consensus from fraying, it errs on the side of repressive order and control over freedom. The system is the opposite of the West's, in which the flaw lies within the strength of diverse participation and competitive elections: a growing inability to forge a governing consensus out of the exploding cacophony of voices and interests. And, as we've seen in the United States on policies ranging from Obamacare to climate change, when all-out competitive partisanship destroys consensus among the body politic, the democratic transfer of power can mean a complete rupture of policies endorsed by most voters only four years earlier. Indeed, the key argument of those who supported the removal of term limits so President Xi can rule indefinitely is the continuity and predictability it will provide of sticking to the course.

In private, even some high-ranking officials lament that the illiberal streak, technocratic bent, connection politics, and corruption of the Communist Party have hollowed out its soul. Not unlike American democracy—with the corrosive influence of money and organized special interests, short-term horizons bound by electoral cycles, and tendency toward gridlock and demagogic politics—China has work to do in conforming its practice to its ideals. Yet it would be a mistake to let its flaws obscure the fundamental features that make China's modern mandarinate work as well as it does.

Whether the removal of the constraints in 2018 of an institutionalized transfer of presidential power makes China's system brittle or stronger depends largely on whether the meritocratic competition of officials, which has been the key for circulating elites and offering critical advice to the ruler, continues to serve as a check on arbitrary initiatives from the top. The prospects of that happening as long as absolute fealty to the man at the helm is demanded are not good. Without robust feedback mechanisms, rulers at the top become insulated from reality. Censorship impedes the ability of the leadership to "seek truth from facts," inviting an illusory construction of what's actually happening on the ground. The problem of "alternative facts" will only deepen if underlings fear the messenger will suffer the consequences of conveying failure or criticism.

At the pinnacle of this system today sits Xi, who some are now calling the Red Emperor. Arguably, Xi has greater power than even Mao. Mao was the all-powerful leader of a weak country; Xi is the all-powerful leader of a country that will soon host the largest economy in the world.

In our first conversation in 2013, Xi was informal and relaxed, sitting at the center of a semicircle of overstuffed chairs that had been set out for us foreign guests. Behind him in the cavernous Great Hall of the People loomed a wall-sized landscape painting of the Great Wall. Xi did not have the stolid technocratic manner that Westerners have so often encountered previously at the top levels in Beijing; instead he conveyed a bracing confidence in his vision and the path on which he was taking his country. The impression he imparted was of a fully formed leader who sees his role as consolidating the historic return of the Middle Kingdom to the center of the world stage; a man who not only believes he is equal to the towering tasks ahead but also is willing to accumulate and wield all the power he can to meet those challenges. He came off as not so much ruthless as unreservedly determined.

His sense of the long history of China, from once-imperial glory to decay and subjugation by the West, was present in everything he said.

Like Deng Xiaoping and Mao before him, Xi peppered his remarks with classical allegories. "As we Chinese say, one needs to read ten thousand books and journey ten thousand miles to gain understanding," he mused at the outset of our first dialogue. "Since China is an ancient civilization with over 5,000 years of history, sometimes we ourselves don't even know where to start. There is a famous poem about Lushan Mountain that says when you view it from different directions you get a different impression. And maybe my own perspective has limitations. As the poem also says, you won't have the whole picture of the mountain when you yourself are on it."

Even so, from his personal vantage point, "we have never been closer," Xi proclaimed, to realizing the Chinese dream of rejuvenation after the long climb back from its humiliation by Great Britain in the Opium Wars 170 years ago. More than anything else China's journey from being on its knees to standing on its feet and now rising to the top ranks of global importance animates the nation's present leadership. One clearly senses the inner confidence among Xi and his colleagues that China's future will be equal to its past as one of the world's great civilizations.

Convinced that China can "avoid the middle-income trap" as a developing country caught in a low-wage export manufacturing economy and meet its goal of doubling per capita income by 2020, Xi predicted the economy would grow for the "next ten to twenty years" at an annual rate of at least 7 percent. This would be possible, he argued, because of ongoing market-oriented structural reforms, accelerated urbanization, and the shift toward innovation and domestic consumption-driven policies. Closing the inequality gap and ending poverty for the 200 million people left behind during the decades of rapid growth are at the top of the agenda, he said.

Raising GDP does not stand alone as a goal, Xi emphasized. Noting that all of China's problems were intertwined and could not be tackled piecemeal, he declared that the "people-centered" reforms he was introducing would be "comprehensive—economic, political, social, and ecological." In short, as Premier Li Keqiang summed up in a separate meeting, China's reform path would shift from a focus on "quantity" to "quality of life."

The new policies Xi outlined, adopted at the Central Committee Plenum the week after our first meeting in 2013, also promised to end labor reeducation camps; ease the one-child policy; rescind the migrant residency requirement in cities that have disallowed incoming rural workers from getting social welfare benefits that remain linked to their birthplace; grant property rights to farmers; and open many new areas of society to a "decisive role" for the market. At the same time, Xi made clear his top priority was "party building"—cleansing the Party of corruption, strengthening its internal discipline, and reasserting its grip on society.

This last pledge Xi has clearly implemented with gusto, snagging high-ranking Communist Party "tigers," such as the powerful former security chief Zhou Yongkang, along with hundreds of others, in his anticorruption net. The task is daunting. As the Politburo member in charge of executing it until 2018, Wang Qishan, put it privately, "It is like a cancer patient operating on himself." Corruption built on the strong ties of *quanxi*— connections and social trust among family and friends—has often proven a far stronger force than law or contracts. Introducing institutions and practices that supplant and break those bonds is no easy matter. In our discussions, we've found that many inside the Party who are deeply uncomfortable with Xi's personalist rule acknowledge that only the strongest hand can purge China of the scourge of pervasive top-to-bottom corruption that threatens to destroy not only the Party but the country. They point out that while Xi's near dictatorial powers bring back horrid memories of the Cultural Revolution, they are aimed at the opposite goal: not instigating chaos to destroy the remnants of Confucian civilization, but rejuvenating a civilization corrupted by the absence of virtue in its governing class. Some called it "a necessary evil."

For Xi, party building also implies consolidating the party's role as the sole organization encompassing all of society. Not long after our first meeting, he launched a campaign of prosecution against human rights lawyers and other civil-society activists who pose even the minutest challenge to Party primacy. He also demanded that the increasingly autonomous media "love the party and protect the party" to ensure that no alternative narrative can challenge its guiding role in society.

In the view of Xi and the other party leaders we met, there is no contradiction between continued liberalization of the economy that opens to the world and greater political and social control. In fact, in their minds, the latter is the condition for the former: lightening up and tightening up are two sides of the same coin.

In this respect, Xi is a true disciple of Deng Xiaoping, the so-called paramount leader who in the late 1970s and 1980s opened China to the global economy. Deng was a pragmatist who continuously calibrated opening up and cracking down to both move forward and maintain stability. His loosened grip on China's economy opened the road to prosperity; his iron fist crushed the Tiananmen Square protests. Xi invoked Deng more than enough to make it clear that he was treading in his footsteps, noting that China was now in the "deep end" of Deng's reforms, which the former leader had said "would last one hundred years." In one notable aspect, of course, Xi departs from Deng, who initiated the system of transfer of power and institutionalized succession through term limits as a way to prevent the return of a personality cult like that of Mao, which resulted in the disastrous Great Leap Forward and Cultural Revolution.

The "Chinese Dream," Xi stressed in that first meeting, could be realized only if China continued to engage in today's interdependent world. "The more developed China becomes," he said, "the more open it will be. It is impossible for China to shut the door that has already been opened." On this score, he said, China was "ready to become more active" in global affairs and to work with other nations to shape new rules of the game. "We will shoulder more international obligations and play a more proactive role in international affairs as well as the reform of the international system," he replied in response to a question from former British prime minister Gordon Brown about China taking on the G-20 chairship, which it subsequently did in 2016. Indeed, by 2017, as President Donald Trump elaborated his "America First" policy with talk of protectionism and the dismantling of trade pacts, Xi emerged as the main defender of globalization at the World Economic Forum, the annual conclave of the global elite in Davos.[6] China, after all, has been the greatest beneficiary of global trade and integration, promoted by all previous US administrations going back to World War II.

Despite the aggressive nationalist tone of the People's Liberation Army generals we met in 2013, and indeed despite Xi's bold assertion of sovereignty a few months later over contested islets in the South and East China seas, Xi invoked the "peaceful rise" doctrine of Zheng Bijian, longtime adviser to China's leadership. The "trend of the times," he told us, is to avoid conflicts inimical to development. Instead China's intends to build "win-win communities of interest on the basis of expanding on the convergence of interests" in areas ranging from open trade to financial stability and battling climate change. Aggression, Xi posited, "is not in the DNA of the country given our long historical and cultural background." He offered this surprising historical reference to Sparta and Athens: "We all need to work together to avoid the Thucydides trap"—destructive tensions between an emerging power and an established power leading to war. The Chinese leaders see taking control of the island chains in the South China Sea not as "aggression" but as building a defense perimeter against an exclusive American-led alliance they see as growing more hostile as China achieves its long climb back to rejuvenation.

By the time we met again in 2015, Xi had considerably bolstered his power. Within a year the Central Committee would elevate him to the role of "core" leader, the status once enjoyed by Deng.[7] Much else had changed as well. The rapid pace of economic growth over the past thirty years that Xi assumed as the foundation of his Chinese Dream had begun to slow markedly by 2015. It was now at what he called a "new normal" of around 6.5 percent—a figure many economists still regard as highly optimistic in the context of a turbulent global economy. Xi remained resolutely positive: pointing to the Thirteenth Five-Year Plan, which had just been announced, he emphasized that China was embarking on an audacious bid to revamp the structure of the entire economy.

The heightened importance that China's leaders attached to convincing the international community of China's capacity for continuing high growth and peaceful intentions was evident throughout our 2015 encounter. Billboards and banners announcing our gathering lined the route from the airport to our conference site. The meeting featured as the top story for two evenings in a row on the main evening news program of CCTV, China's state-run television station. In a sign of the weight Xi assigned to our dialogue, he brought along key members of his inner circle, including his chief of staff, Li Zhanshu, and Party theorist Wang Huning—both of whom were later elevated to the seven-member Standing Committee of the Politburo, which rules China. Also present were Foreign Minister Wang Yi and State Councilor Yang Jiechi.

The tenor and format this time suggested more a working conference than an audience with the emperor. We sat in a less cavernous room, around a horseshoe-shaped set of tables with name placards. The backdrop was a mural of the Forbidden City amid modern-day Beijing. President Xi sat at the center. After opening comments, he listened to remarks by several former heads of state and government—Ernesto Zedillo of Mexico, Goh Chok Tong of Singapore, and Kevin Rudd of Australia, as well as former US treasury secretary Lawrence Summers. Xi took notes and responded. He agreed with Summers's statement that China can't grow unless the world economy does, and the world economy can't grow without China. China was cognizant of its responsibilities, Xi said. It was doing its part by setting up the Asian Infrastructure Investment Bank and making commitments to develop infrastructure across Eurasia to Africa as part of the revived Silk Road trading and commerce routes—the so-called "One Belt, One Road" project—from Beijing to Istanbul and on to Africa, which is one of Xi's top priorities. Xi assured Singapore's Goh Chok Tong that China would be sensitive to concerns expressed by smaller nations along the route that local economies benefit from the initiative and not just serve as outlets for China's industrial overproduction. Facial expressions around the table expressed doubts on this score.

The blueprint for China's future, embodied in the Five-Year Plan Xi outlined, signals the most momentous shift in direction since the death of Mao and the advent of Deng Xiaoping's reforms and opening-up in 1978. Vice-Premier Zhang Gaoli, the Politburo Standing Committee member in charge of the economy at the time, laid out for us the plan's comprehensive dimensions. Zhang envisions upgrading China's manufacturing and infrastructure via the resource and logistical efficiency enabled by the "internet of things"—what the Chinese call Internet Plus. He spoke of "circular" use of resources in which waste is recycled, and about "weakening the urban concentration of Beijing" by building decentralized, smart infrastructure in the northern provinces surrounding the capital. Under the new plan, he said, a top criterion in the promotion evaluations of mayors, governors, and party secretaries will be their "green" accomplishments in protecting the environment and promoting clean energy.

Zhang enunciated a mantra that has been on the lips of every cadre and bureaucrat in every corner of China since: the nation, he said, was embracing "innovation" and "mass entrepreneurship." Although it is questionable how fully Communist Party apparatchiks grasp the meaning of these words in any practical sense, the mantra nonetheless reflects the recognition by Xi and his colleagues that the export-manufacturing model that has resulted in the high growth rates of past decades due to massive inputs of labor and capital has about run out of steam. New wealth and sustained growth, they now understand, can come only from the revitalization of industry through the application of information technology.

Slogans, of course, don't make an economic revolution. Nobel economist Michael Spence, who has advised China on its economic plans, warily remarked to the group that in the history of economic development, "there is no precedent for the scale and scope of what China is now trying to accomplish." The big question about the great leap forward proposed by China's leaders is whether innovation can be planned, and just how far they are willing to go in giving "a decisive role to the market" as the vital spur to "mass" entrepreneurship. And the more the market plays a role, the more China's economy will experience pronounced business cycles—booms and busts instead of uninterrupted growth.

China's high-tech successes offer clear evidence of the entrepreneurial genius of Chinese society. Baidu, a search engine not unlike Google, is one of the world's biggest internet companies. Alibaba, an e-commerce site, is the Chinese version of Amazon. Indeed, Reid Hoffman, a cofounder of LinkedIn and a top venture capitalist, observed at the meeting that Chinese start-ups have an edge over Silicon Valley entrepreneurs because "they work much harder and will do anything to win." To promote innovation, the state heavily subsidizes start-ups through a variety of mechanisms including free rent and tax breaks during the early years of a firm's development, as well as low-cost loans from state banks. China filed more patents in 2015 than any other country. And, through an initiative called World Class 2.0, it is seeking to make six major Chinese universities among the top in the world by 2020. It's "Made in China 2025" effort seeks to conquer the latest technologies from electric cars to semiconductors within the decade. In July 2017, China's state council announced an ambitious endeavor to make China the world leader in artificial intelligence by 2030.[8]

If the past few decades are prologue, there is reason to believe China will reach the last-mentioned goal. "China has an edge in its ability to combine strong, top-down government directive with vibrant grassroots-level innovation," notes Edward Tse, the Shanghai-based management guru. "Beyond this, China has an abundance of data to train AI-learning algorithms because of its huge population of Internet users—more than 700 million. China's thriving mobile Internet ecosystem also provides a test bed for AI researchers to collect and analyze valuable demographics and transactional and behavioral big data and to conduct large-scale experiments at a much higher level and greater speed than foreign counterparts."[9] Alphabet/Google's Eric Schmidt, for one who should know, believes that China will catchup with the United States in AI development by the end of 2018.

Can "Internet Plus" and "Internet Minus" Go Together?

But there is a profound contradiction for the Communist Party as it seeks to shift from the second industrial revolution of smokestack manufacturing to the third industrial revolution, based on information technology: innovation entails steady disruption, whereas the Party seeks above all to maintain stability. It is not easy to see how China can clamp down and "purify" the internet by limiting the flow of information, as Xi has called for, while also extolling "Internet Plus" innovation. Can "Internet Plus" and "Internet Minus" go together? As we pointed out to China's internet czar at the time, Lu Wei, where Chinese authorities decide to draw the line between "freedom" and "order" will determine the scope of innovation-based prosperity.

The part of China's ambitions involving the integration of smart technology and infrastructure is more likely to be realized effectively. That strategy benefits from the long-term continuity of policy and purpose that has been one of the one-party system's strengths. The Thirteenth Five-Year Plan marks only the beginning of the transition that China's economic managers hope to complete through the Made in China 2025 initiative.[10] Germany has a similar plan to integrate the internet into industry, called Industry 4.0.[11] Indeed, Chancellor Angela Merkel was visiting Beijing when we were there in 2015, signing agreements with Premier Li Keqiang to bolster coordination between the two manufacturing powers.[12] Here Germany and China clearly have an edge on the United States, which has plenty of mass entrepreneurship but precious little political capacity to build out the infrastructure of the future.

The road ahead for China is not likely to be smooth. President Xi sees Made in China 2025 as rocket fuel for the rejuvenation of the Chinese nation, which he is determined to keep from falling behind the West as it did during the Ming and Qing dynasties of the late nineteenth century. Trade hawks in the United States, on the other hand, see Made in China 2025 as an existential threat to America's technological supremacy, and all that it implies in terms of military might and geopolitical sway. Indeed, of all the contested issues between the United States and China, technology is most likely to spring the Thucydides trap.[13]

China faces other challenges as well in the transition ahead. To stimulate faltering growth in recent years, it has unleashed vast amounts of credit into the economy, creating overcapacity in real estate and elsewhere.[14] The massive, empty apartment buildings one used to associate with second- and third-tier cities in China are now plentiful even around primary cities like Beijing. And the large state-owned industries lack discipline when it comes to spending. By some estimates, the resulting national debt ratio is more than 260 percent of GDP.[15]

This debt-fueled effort to sustain economic growth was deemed necessary because of slackening demand in the global economy, demand on which China's export model has depended. As Xi acknowledged in his response to Larry Summers, China is now embedded in the global market. But debt-stimulated growth cannot long substitute for export markets or real innovation in industry. No doubt aware of this conundrum, by 2017 the Chinese authorities had begun implementing a range of measures to curb credit expansion, including cracking down on the easy-money empires that so-called Gray Rhinos amassed by buying up foreign assets, and reining in loose local government spending.

In our 2015 conversation, President Xi pinned his hopes on the G-20, whose summit he would chair the following year. As Xi put it, he wanted to "cement" the role of the G-20 as the premier governing body able to coordinate common policies to foster global growth. When the G-20 convened in September 2016, he reiterated this point while proposing a path for shared development that mirrored China's own Five-Year Plan and its "One Belt, One Road" initiative to revive the old Silk Road routes. To emphasize the importance of innovation as a key means of wealth creation, the summit of world leaders was held in Hangzhou, the hometown of Jack Ma and headquarters of Alibaba—the foremost emblem of China's third industrial revolution.

Fred Hu, one of China's leading economists and a member of the 21st Century Council, argues that the shift toward a more consumer-centric and innovation-led economy is already under way. According to Hu, a former International Monetary Fund economist, consumption accounted for "over 50 percent of overall GDP growth in 2014 and 60 percent in the first half of 2015.

While top line GDP growth has been trending down, growth," he says, "is now broader-based in a much larger economy than a decade ago; also more balanced, higher quality and possibly more environmentally friendly—if only judging by the increasing count of blue sky days in Beijing."[16]

For Hu, growth rates moderating into the range of 5–7 percent per annum reflect higher per capita income and the changing growth pattern in China. As he sees it, "a modest slowdown is a necessary and healthy adjustment for China to transition to a new trajectory of more efficient and sustainable growth." Hu suggests a set of reforms to help smooth the transition, including tax and credit incentives for first-time home buyers, broader health and social security coverage, and financial aid to students in vocational schools—in short, policies that channel financial resources from industry to the household. Above all, he proposes investment in "environmental infrastructure," which presently suffers from "woeful underinvestment" in China.

Although an economic slowdown is likely unavoidable as China's economic model lurches from heavy investment in industry and exports to domestic consumption and greater household income, it has nonetheless dented confidence in the sense of omnicompetence upon which the Communist Party's legitimacy has been based.

The Chinese scholar Yao Yang has made the case for a "disinterested," no-party or "one party" system as the best governing arrangement for inclusive growth in the developing world.[17] He sees what he calls "disinterested government" as the common element that has enabled democracies such as South Korea and Taiwan, as well as more authoritarian states like Singapore and China, to collectively achieve "the Asian miracle" of rapid economic development. He cites Mancur Olson's idea of an "encompassing organization" that represents the interests of the whole society instead of favoring either an elite kleptocracy or populist redistribution schemes that the level of growth can't afford.[18] The aim of government is to lift all boats and service all of society.

While Yao is no doubt correct that an encompassing organization can effectively plan out the capital and labor inputs for low-wage manufacturing for export in a growing global economy, how will the same "disinterested" development approach fare in the face of the tumultuous disruptions of the Digital Age? Nobel Laureate Joseph Stiglitz once remarked to us that markets are not good at big economic and technological transitions. The great experiment in which China is now engaged will reveal whether the political management of such change by an encompassing one-party system is any more successful.

Take the Slogans Seriously

The Nineteenth Party Congress, held in November 2017, affirmed the path Xi had outlined in our two meetings. It even enshrined his goals in the constitution as "Xi Jinping Thought," thus placing him on historic par with Mao.

For Westerners, the promotion of "Xi Jinping Thought on Socialism with Chinese Characteristics for the New Era" and the wooden Party-speak slogans repeated ad nauseam causes our eyes to glaze over and numbs our minds. We tend to dismiss such corny formulations as empty rhetoric with a distinctly Orwellian ring. But in China's Marxist-Leninist-Confucian ensemble, they do serve as rallying points for unifying a vast body politic and moving it forward. They do set out the orientation and time-lined expectations of society, even for those—and there are many—who make fun of the turgid liturgy with which they are continually bombarded.

Add up all the mass slogans and you get a pretty good picture of where China is headed in the "new era" it now proclaims: "Great rejuvenation of the Chinese nation"; "a socialist market economy with Chinese characteristics"; "mass entrepreneurship"; "a moderately prosperous society in all respects by 2020"; "socialist modernization by 2035 that brings a prosperous, strong, democratic, culturally advanced, harmonious and beautiful country by the middle of this century." Lately, "ecological civilization" has been added to the mix. And, of course, above all, "uphold the Party's guidance, keep to the Party's direction of progress, and maintain the Party's lofty will." On the global front, slogans include "the Belt and Road initiative inaugurates the next phase of globalization that promises a new foundation for shared global growth"; "a new type of great power relationship"; and "a community of a shared future."

One can see how these orienting slogans frame the agenda in much the same way as they do in democratic election campaigns. Think of Obama's "Yes We Can" or Trump's "Make America Great Again." In China, as in the West, they also serve as a benchmark with which to judge whether actions meet words. The huge difference is that, in China, a disciplined Party carries them out over decades without a break in the continuity of its rule.

Behind China's Fear of a "Color Revolution"

In our discussions on the sidelines of the meeting with Xi in 2015, the challenges the party faced were evident on many fronts. We heard a firsthand report on the intensive anticorruption campaign from a leading member of the Party's Discipline Inspection Commission. With the vice-president of the Supreme People's Court, we had an opportunity to candidly debate the difference between Western-style "rule of law," according to which an independent judiciary protects citizens, and China's "rule by law," whereby the judiciary is effectively an extension of the Party. Former Swedish prime minister Carl Bildt, now head of the Global Commission on Internet Governance, sparred with then–internet czar Lu Wei over China's "internet sovereignty" policy, which seeks to control information once it flows in across China's borders. Bildt called instead for China to adopt a "one net, one world" policy in the same spirit it has called for "One Belt, One Road."

The consistent message we took away in our meetings was that in the face of all the challenges of "rejuvenation"—corruption, pollution, economic inequality, mass internal migration, the explosion of technology giving everyone access to the same information—Xi has dug in his heels, placing all bets on the ability of a disciplined party to encompass all of society's interests and see his nation through. Left unspoken but implicit in all that we heard as "foreign guests" was Xi's firm belief, shared by his inner circle, that the Western democracies are out to weaken China by undermining its only practical hope—the continuing dominance of the Communist Party with Xi at the helm. Unless the West learns to appreciate this mindset—of the rulers certainly, but also of much, if not the preponderant majority, of the population—according to which China's continuing success is seen as inextricably bound up with the Party's rule, it will badly misread the forces shaping the foreseeable future.

The summer after our 2015 meeting, in August 2016, China convicted several lawyers of "subversion" for colluding with "foreign forces" (read: the United States) in mounting legal challenges to the state. The lawyers' alleged aim had been to foment regime change in Beijing like the popular uprisings of the Arab Spring and the "color revolutions" against autocrats in Ukraine (so called because orange was the color of banners and other symbols employed by the opposition). In what were clearly forced performances, some of the accused confessed on television that their actions had opened doors to the deleterious influence of Western ideas. To hammer home that message in conjunction with the trials, the chief prosecutor's office, the Supreme People's Procuratorate, released a video showing the chaos, violence, and instability in regions around the world where the West has sought to promote democracy, mostly in the Middle East and North Africa, conveying to Chinese viewers that the stability they enjoy is due to China's one-party system. It is likely the video was well received. According to a recent Pew Survey, 77 percent of Chinese polled believe their way of life must be protected against "foreign influence."[19]

Despite what many in the top ranks of power in Beijing clearly seem to think, regime change is not an active US policy. Sources tell us that when Barack Obama was president, he sought to disabuse Xi of this notion both in person and in a detailed letter. Specifically, he addressed Beijing's charge that the United States was fomenting student agitation for Western-style elections and independence in Hong Kong. Xi was not convinced; he believes there is a deep-seated ideological expectation among America's political class that China's governing system is "on the wrong side of history," as Bill Clinton once put it, and destined to fail.[20]

Former Australian prime minister Kevin Rudd has cited this issue as a perennial obstacle in relations between the world's two largest economies. The Chinese have concluded, he wrote in a report for the Belfer Center at Harvard, "that the United States has not, and never will, accept the fundamental political legitimacy of the Chinese administration because it is not a liberal democracy."[21] Fu Ying, until 2018 the powerful chair of the Foreign Affairs Committee of the National People's Congress, confirmed this point from the Chinese side. "The West will never accept that we are reforming until we have a Gorbachev," she told us in Beijing. For China's leaders, Mikhail Gorbachev's freeing of the media and unleashing of democratic reforms led inevitably to the collapse of the Soviet party and state.

President Donald Trump's initial realpolitik, transactional, deal-making mindset no doubt was perceived with relief by China's leaders. Yet their highly attuned sense of civilizational pride—combined with the Trump administration's headlong launch of a trade war and formal declaration that China is a "strategic rival"—tells them that the animus of Western democracies endures. Indeed, vice-president Pence's speech in October 2017, widely regarded as the touchstone of a new Cold War with its call to contain China and promote more personal liberty and religious freedom, confirmed this view. China's leaders thus remain both reactive to what they see as outsiders trying to change their system and proactive in insisting on its legitimacy.

This issue of political legitimacy shadows every aspect of Western, and particularly US, relations with China. It constrains any fuller embrace between the two powers and raises suspicions over every initiative. As long as the Chinese see a threat, they will continue to inveigh against "Western values"; fearing subversion, they will continue to crack down on lawyers and human rights activists. That, in turn, only reinforces Western perceptions that China's system is inherently repressive and must be challenged. Absent acknowledgement of a "symmetry of validity" that would change the narrative, this destructive cycle of symbiotic antagonism will continue and a Cold War taste will sour the idea of any new relationship in the times ahead. To be sure, the advent of Xi's personalist rule so fundamentally challenges Western notions of governance that it deepens the fissure.

The Chinese, who remember the wounds of imperialism as though inflicted yesterday, would less defensively and less resentfully accept criticism at home or from abroad—for example, that censorship impedes the "seek truth from facts" pragmatism that has guided reform efforts since Deng Xiaoping—if the criticism were rooted in a basic recognition of legitimacy and therefore not seen as a ruse, plot, or conspiracy to overturn their system of governance. Europeans, after all, regularly criticize US policies on gun rights and urban racial strife and the high US prison population. Americans regularly criticize Europe's inability to assimilate immigrants. Such criticisms are always annoying to those on the receiving end, but are taken in stride because they are not seen as assaults on the foundations of one another's political systems.

The Communist regime's repressive tendencies already fit within its Marxist-Leninist-Confucian mindset of control. The incessant pressure from the West that China change its ways offers only a further justification to clamp down colored by nationalist sentiments.

The Crackdown on "Civil Society"

Xi's enforcement efforts—his campaigns against corruption as well as his intensifying crackdown on dissidents and activists—are rooted in a traditional conception of the respective roles of the central state, society, and the individual that, for millennia, has sustained the unbroken continuity of Chinese culture. To understand the historical resonances of what scholar Pan Wei calls China's "institutional civilization" is not in any way to justify or absolve repression.[22] Particularly egregious violations of human rights, such as the atrocious treatment of the dying dissident and Nobel Peace laureate Liu Xiaobo in his waning days in 2017, demonstrate a brutality unjustified by any standards, Western or Eastern, just as Xi's personalist rule violates any constitutional standards, West or East, of restraint on absolute power. But understanding China's historical trajectory does dispel Western critics' self-righteous illusion that change can be imposed from the outside. The Western ideal of a free-for-all civil society and competitive elections is not for everyone, especially as they have shown their darker side in the age of social media and populism. And even if such ideals are considered universal, nations don't progress everywhere at the same pace or on the same track. Change establishes itself only if owned by those who make it.

Because it has largely delivered on its promises in recent decades, the Chinese Communist Party has attracted, by the accounts of even Western pollsters, the allegiance of most of its population—making China far from the fertile ground for revolt by a discontented populace that some in the West seem to imagine. Although cynical attitudes toward the Party's overbearing paternalism can easily be found, a Pew study in 2013 showed nonetheless that more than 80 percent of Chinese polled said their country was headed in the right direction. (In the same poll, only 31 percent of Americans felt the same way about the United States' trajectory.)[23] A 2015 poll reported that 77 percent of Chinese surveyed said they were better off than five years before, despite major concerns about pollution and official corruption.[24] Such numbers suggest that, for now at least, the Party has achieved what Antonio Gramsci, the Italian communist political theorist of the turn of the twentieth century, called "ideological hegemony."[25]

Long before Harvard's Joseph Nye came up with his distinction between "soft power" and "hard power," Gramsci wrote of two different kinds of hegemony, or dominance.[26] For Gramsci, the hegemony of the state is rooted in force: to impose and maintain order in society, the state must establish a monopoly over the means of violence. But hegemony in "civil society" must be based on consent—hearts and minds. Allegiance to a common worldview and values must be earned and cannot be forced; the public must buy into a governing narrative voluntarily, or the narrative, by definition, lacks legitimacy. For Gramsci, it is such soft power that legitimates hard power, not vice versa. Gramsci therefore envisioned his Italian Communist Party as part of civil society, not the state. The party would gain state power, he believed, only by convincing civil society of its narrative.

The sharp distinction that Gramsci outlines between civil society and the state never developed historically in China. The Middle Kingdom never experienced the contest between religious and political authority, each carving out its autonomous space, that is a hallmark of the history of the West. China has always had a unitary state encompassing all of society, with no distinct realm outside its fold.[27]

In today's China, the party-state has merged the two forms of hegemony that Gramsci outlined, blurring the roles of force and consent in maintaining power.

The related absence of any enduring tradition of the separation of powers also shapes the current debates in China over an independent judiciary. The School of Legalism of the Qin dynasty (221–206 BCE)—said to be President Xi's primary inspiration in his anticorruption campaign—aimed to affirm the administrative power of the unitary state.[28] Its rule-by-law philosophy was meant to ensure that rulers and citizens alike obeyed the laws set forth by the state whenever the ethical imperatives that Confucianism spells out for personal rectitude fall short. Unlike the West's rule-of-law tradition, Legalism was never meant to provide the individual a way to redress abuses of power through an appeal to an independent judiciary. It is more about the regulation of society by the state.

Inclusive Hegemony

The Singapore-based Chinese scholar Zheng Yongnian offers the best description of how all of this works out in practice. As he points out, the development of a civil sphere in China has been like nothing one would have seen in the West. He characterizes it as a "dual process of legitimation and domination" that has mutually transformed both the Communist Party and civil society. By "taking into account the interests of other social forces and linking them with its own," Zheng writes, the Party itself has necessarily been "self-transformed," creating a kind of systemic accountability.[29] The Australian China scholar John Keane even argues that China is a kind of "phantom democracy" in which, paradoxically, "the fear of democracy forces a style of political management that in many ways mirrors and mimics electoral democracies, where the fear of elections puts leaders in constant campaign mode."[30]

This two-way dynamic has its roots in the traditional Confucian ethos of governance. In contrast to the modern Western ethos according to which the consent of the governed grants legitimacy, legitimacy in the traditional Confucian perspective is rooted in the virtue of the ruler. He is bound in a reciprocal relationship with his subjects, serving their needs as they obey his commands. In the *Analects,* Confucius lays out the mutual obligations of the virtuous hierarchical order: "If a man is correct in his own person, then there will be obedience without orders being given. But if he is not correct in his own person, there will not be obedience even though orders are given."

This dynamic of responsiveness for sustaining legitimacy is at the core of the "adaptive authoritarianism" and "inclusive hegemony" that have enabled the Party to survive in China through pragmatic accommodation of policies to changing realities. Policies change, but the Party system, like the emperor system for millennia before it, does not. Thus, the Party has continuously morphed from a peasant organization dominated by Mao at its founding into the broad social tent it is today with more than 90 million members, including even billionaires professing Buddhism.[31]

The result is a kind of fuzzy-power arrangement in which there is mutual dependence between the party-state and the people. The party-state is like a utility shaped by its users. As an encompassing service provider, its legitimacy derives from its capacity to deliver the goods and respond to social concerns. If it doesn't respond to the broad will of the people, the ideological hegemony that cements the Party's power will come unglued. The system's legitimacy is diminished to the extent that force, including censorship, substitutes for consent. What has made China's one-party system work so far will fail in the future if repression replaces adaptation and if hegemony is enforced from the top instead of legitimated through inclusiveness from below.

From this perspective, the present course China is taking is indeed worrying. The removal of constraints on the institutional transfer of power, the insertion of "Xi Jinping Thought" into the Chinese constitution, and the transmutation of digital connectivity into a potentially totalitarian system of surveillance of 1.4 billion people ring every alarm bell. Everything now depends on the quality of meritocratic competition within the Party—in effect, checks and balances with Chinese characteristics—that can temper or resist misguided initiative from the top, as well as on the robustness of feedback loops at all government levels and from netizens across the Web. Absent those correctives, what has been effective governance in China could become so brittle as to break when crisis hits, as it inevitably will.

The exercise of fuzzy power that relies on the floating balance of power in society often means arbitrary imposition and shifting of red lines that can't be crossed. Thus, the artist Ai Weiwei is proudly provided with the permits needed to build a studio, only to have the studio later bulldozed by the same authorities. One day he is jailed and beaten, then put under house arrest and his passport taken away. The next day he is given back his passport and allowed to display his political art in high-profile exhibitions in Europe. In March 2015 a privately produced video criticizing China's pollution was allowed to go viral on YouKu, China's version of YouTube. But once it became "too viral" and authorities began to realize they will be as much blamed for creating an unlivable environment as credited with trying to clean it up, the video was censored.[32]

An Emerging Autonomous Civil Society?

A sharpening definition of this fuzziness in China's system of power, however, appears to be in the works as an autonomous sphere for civil society of the kind associated with the West may be emerging. The system that has managed to balance stability and change for so long is being challenged as never before.

What is different for China now than it was during its more than two thousand years of institutional civilization is the intrusion of the Information Age, in which all more or less share access to the same information as their rulers have despite the broad, hit-and-miss censorship practices. And it is here that the guiding anxiety of China's top party officials, who are determined not to succumb to the fate of the Soviet Communist Party, appears misplaced. They are laboring under the power of the wrong metaphor.

As Xi and his colleagues see it, the Soviet party met its demise because of Gorbachev's policy of glasnost, or transparent information. They have thus concluded the way to survive is to construct a narrative people are compelled to believe by controlling what they are otherwise allowed to know. The reality is that the Soviet party collapsed precisely because of a similar effort to *disguise* reality with a narrative that didn't square with people's actual experience. When the lies were taken away under glasnost, there was nothing there.

The Chinese Party could not be more different. In China the emperor does have clothes. The Party has demonstrably delivered for its people over the past three decades precisely by following the pragmatic dictum of "seeking truth from facts" instead of spinning reality. What saved China from the disastrous years of Maoist policies was Deng Xiaoping's insistence on taking the ideological blinders off, acknowledging real facts on the ground, and accepting the incentives of self-interest and self-improvement that drive people. For Deng, whose famous dictum was "Black cat, white cat, what does it matter as long as it catches the rat," organizing society in such a way was the only hope of achieving results.

Admitting mistakes—brought to government officials' attention by the activists and social media of a fledging civil society—and fixing them, not covering them up, is what establishes legitimacy in the Information Age, when everyone knows what's what anyway. The old system of hierarchical control that could once impose an authoritative narrative is doomed by the democratization of information. Just as the bourgeoisie created the space for civil society vis-à-vis royal absolutism in Europe, and just as women are today the makers of a democratic public sphere vis-à-vis theocracy and patriarchy in the Islamic world, so, too, social networks and media are the makers of civil society in today's China.

In a conversation in March 2015 China's then–internet czar, Lu Wei, quite openly acknowledged that, absent competitive elections, robust feedback through free expression on weibo or WeChat (China's Twitter-like microblogs) and other media is a necessary corrective to authority. No one in the leadership misses the fact that, with hundreds of millions of netizens, China's cybersphere is the new Tiananmen Square of modern times. While the authorities seek to balance free expression on the Web, they also fully recognize that the Web will necessarily balance the government—and, indeed, is a key mechanism of "sousveillance," or monitoring from below by the public, especially when it comes to corruption and official accountability. (In one telling episode in Beijing, one of the authors met for lunch with a high-ranking official. When the meal was over, the official instructed her aide: "Take all the leftovers in case someone snaps a photo with their phone and posts on weibo that ranking cadres are living high on the hog and wasting food.")

The fact that China's party-state is now spending $182 billion to boost internet speeds by 2020 means that it is either digging its own grave by giving the masses a gigantic platform for expressing discontent if it can't deliver, or laying the ground for a new type of monitory infrastructure that will shift the political balance between state and netizen by enhancing the system's adaptive capacity.[33]

All these developments are new and unprecedented for such an old civilization. Whether China ends up on the wrong side of history or not depends on its ability to find a balance between rule from the top and an emergent civil society from below. To be sure, the authorities in China are doubling their efforts, having cracked down in the summer of 2017 on virtual private networks (VPNs) used by many research institutes, scholars, and foreign companies to stay connected to the world beyond the censors who police internet sovereignty. Liu Binjie, China's former top censor and now a member of the National People's Congress, thinks the "Great Firewall," not to mention its extension to VPN, is unsustainable. Others, like historian Zhang Lifan, hold that there will be no going back, that extended censorship is here to stay.[34]

In China, as elsewhere—though more so because of its "institutional civilization"—there is a dark side. Where there is connectivity there is also surveillance, as we learned from Edward Snowden's revelations of the NSA global spying programs. Google, Facebook, and other data companies trace a person's online profile in order to sell information on consumers' daily habits and tastes to marketers. While such commercial enterprises intrude into people's privacy in the West, in China the government intrudes further. One of the most ominous developments in China today is the construction of a nationwide big-data collection and analysis system. On the positive side, the project would make business practices, food safety, and official behavior transparent to the consumer—realizing the potential of a two-way watchdog.[35] By 2020, government data is due to open to the public in twenty-plus civil welfare and benefits-related areas, including transportation, social security, and natural resources. The ominous aspect involves giving all citizens a "social credit" score based on blended metrics that could include everything from a neighbor's report that a person littered on the street, to shopping addictions, to an offhand comment expressing disloyalty to the Party-run state. The totalitarian potential is all too evident.

In the years ahead, China is unlikely to take many cues from the West. But it might take a cue from Singapore, its soft-authoritarian cousin that holds dear many of the Confucian values that China does. When the encompassing umbrella of the banyan tree becomes so dense it shuts out too much light to allow new growth on the ground beneath, Singapore's former foreign minister George Yeo has written, it needs to be pruned.[36] Having earned the people's allegiance to its narrative through performance, Singapore's nanny state has gained the confidence to lighten up and give the emergent civil society more room to breathe. Indeed, in the September 2015 elections in that tropical city-state, the People's Action Party, which has ruled since independence in 1965, actually increased its share in the parliament. Indicative of the times, the always–ahead of the curve former dean of the Lee Kuan Yew School of Public Policy Kishore Mahbubani, has made "participation" the new focus of study in the post-Lee era.[37]

China's leaders would better serve their cause by adopting the power of the apt metaphor from their own civilizational sphere—Singapore—instead of remaining rigid to the point of brittleness and obsessing about the collapse of the old Soviet party, which has little in common with the Asian way.

This battle will have to be fought out within China by those at the intersection of an open and closing world. We in the West should encourage China's effort to forge a new equilibrium out of its own experience, not seek to project our legacy with all its faults onto its future. Our only relevant contribution to fostering more freedom in China would be to demonstrate through our own institutional innovations how inclusive politics and a governing consensus can be achieved by other than authoritarian means.

Charting an Alternative World Order

At least rhetorically, President Xi maintains that China does not want to "overturn" the existing order and build an alternative global system, but rather, as he told us, to "complement" the present institutions that have served the world well—above all, multilateral forums like the United Nations and the World Trade Organization (WTO). At the Berggruen Institute's second "Understanding China" conference in Beijing in November 2015, Fu Ying, at that time the National People's Congress foreign affairs committee chair, made a similar case setting out China's vision of global order: "The current international order, although imperfect in its efficiency and execution, is the closest to fairness that mankind has achieved," she said. "It does however, need to be improved, using the wisdom and drive of all its members to bring about change. China has reaffirmed that it has no intention of creating a parallel order, but rather it would like to see a 'world of nations' under the same roof, big enough to house all countries."

Where China departs from the West, she argues, is in the security realm. "China has been ostracized by the Western military coalition, with its values dismissed as being 'alien' to the US led world order. To safeguard its own security and stability," Fu continued, "China has been wary of the political and security agenda promoted by the West. However, over recent years, its growing strength has given China more authority and influence internationally, enabling China to join the efforts promoting more balanced global development through long overdue reforms and improvements. However, this has caused unfounded suspicion by some that China's departure from its longtime passive posture is a sign of it challenging the US led world order." Alluding to the so-called Thucydides trap to which Xi referred, in which rising powers inevitably clash with established powers, she warns: "World history shows that order does not evolve in a linear way. Over time, old orders have given way to new ones due to clashes among major powers or through the decline of the superior power. A successful order should be able to accommodate the growing interests of all its members."

On this score, China is hedging its bets. As NATO is being fortified as an alliance against Russia's newfound assertiveness in Ukraine and has officially declared both China and Russia as "strategic rivals," China is taking a leading role with Russia in consolidating a new anti-Western league through the Shanghai Cooperation Council. It also spares no effort in bilateral approaches designed to wean American allies, such as the Philippines, from the US orbit. Even though a United Nations tribunal arbitrating the Convention on the Law of the Sea ruled in favor of the Philippines in 2016 and nullified China's claims, China nonetheless pushes on.[38] In a sign of China's growing clout, Philippine president Rodrigo Duterte has not pushed back. On the contrary, Duterte canceled various joint military exercises with the United States in the South China Sea, while nixing initial plans for joint patrols in the area. In exchange, China has offered a multibillion-dollar package of infrastructure investment and a 500 million–dollar loan to the Philippine military.[39]

China is hedging its bets as well by plotting out an alternative economic order. As we discussed with President Xi, it has established the Asian Infrastructure Investment Bank and launched a trillion-dollar infrastructure investment initiative to revitalize the ancient Silk Road trading routes of Pax Mongolica, established in the thirteenth and fourteenth centuries. While the United States retrenches as the main driver of globalization under President Trump, China is barreling ahead, seeking to tie together the world from the Far East across Eurasia to Africa and Europe.

Zheng Bijian, a top Party strategist and member of the Berggruen Institute's 21st Century Council, sees what China calls the One Belt, One Road initiative as the vanguard of "a new phase of globalization" that seeks to promote "the spirit of a 'community of common destiny for all mankind' through a more balanced distribution of existing and innovative forces of wealth production." In terms of purchasing power parity, Zheng explains, "the size of developed economies as a whole versus that of the developing economies as a whole was at a ratio of 64:36 in 1980 and 50:50 in 2007. In 2018, this ratio is expected to reverse to 41:59, tipping the scales toward the developing world." If this trend can be sustained," he continues, "it means that the global economy as a whole, driven by the developing world, will continue to gather new momentum for growth in the second, third and fourth decades of this century. The more rapid growth in the developing economies will in turn stimulate renewed growth in the developed world by becoming an even larger market for its goods and services. The new phase of globalization will thus be a reverse from the past in which the developed world was the growth engine." By investing massively in infrastructure across these regions, Zheng argues, China can boost that growth potential to everyone's benefit.[40]

Both Fu Ying's idea of "all nations under one roof" and Zheng Bijian's notion of "a community of common destiny for all mankind" have deep roots in China's cultural history. The philosopher Zhao Tingyang has revived the ancient concept from the Zhou dynasty three thousand years ago of *tianxia*—"all under heaven" coexisting in harmony—in current debates over China's role in the world. The Zhou dynasty, Zhao notes, "sought to bring the whole world together under one tent as a way to eliminate any negative external influence, and thereby conflict, within what was then considered the civilized world." *Tianxia*, he says, "defines the concept of 'the political' as the art of co-existing through transforming hostility into hospitality—a clear alternative to the more modern concepts of German legal theorist Carl Schmitt's recognition of politics as 'us vs. them,' Hans Morgenthau's 'realist' struggle for power and Samuel Huntington's 'clash of civilizations.'"[41]

The philosophical basis of the *tianxia* concept, Zhao explains, is the Confucian notion of "live and let live," which seeks to minimize conflict instead of maximizing self-interest. For Zhao, such a mode of coexistence is the most rational formula for peace and stability in today's diverse world. "A 'tianxia peace' for our hyper-connected, interdependent world ... would have to be built on the broader foundation of a compatible universalism that includes all civilizations—not an exclusive unilateral claim of one civilization to universality."[42]

Other scholars point out that China's "nonuniversalist" worldview is better suited to building a harmonious and inclusive global order going forward than Western universalism. Zhang Xianglong, of Beijing University's philosophy department, argues that a "clash of civilizations" or the "end of history" can "only occur when universalist cultures encounter each other or prevail over each other. When two non-universalist cultures meet there may well be friction, but total warfare that aims at mutual annihilation is generally avoided. When, however, two universalist cultures meet, even though they may compromise and negotiate to ensure their temporary safety, in the long run they are in principle engaged in a to-the-death struggle." Indeed, Zhang notes, Buddhism and Taoism coexisted for millennia in China. Tan Chung, who for many years was the dean of the Centre for East Asian Studies at Jawaharlal Nehru University and headed the Delhi Institute for Chinese Studies, viewed the 2008 Olympics in Beijing as significant not just as the coming-out party for the new China but also for the reappearance of the Confucian sensibility in world affairs. "The magnificent success of the Beijing Olympics," he said at the time, "objectively marked the transition of the world from the 'geopolitical paradigm' to the 'geo-civilizational paradigm' in which China takes the lead." In Tan's view, China, consistent with its history, is not interested in "maximizing power through the conquest of territory or ideological space like a superpower, but in the integration of civilizations through harmonious coexistence." He even argues that "all the brilliant ancient civilizations [of the West] like Babylonia, Egypt, Greece and Rome have become ruins without being handed down. This was because there was no 'geo-civilizational paradigm' among them. The 'geopolitical paradigm' pushed them to scramble for space and indulge in mutual destruction. The basic difference between Eastern and Western hemispheres lies here."[43]

These somewhat idealized versions of China's ancient history now face the test of our contemporary times. Harmony may work if other nations act as subordinate tributaries to the Middle Kingdom. Where they are wont to go their own way, or do not see their interests as consonant with China's, discord is more likely.

"China now appears to be changing from an adapter to a driver of globalization," adds economist Stephen Roach. "In effect, the Next China is upping the ante on its connection to an increasingly integrated world—and creating a new set of risks and opportunities along the way." Present interests always give specific shape to worldviews, no matter how deeply grounded in cultural history. Roach sees the One Belt, One Road initiative not only as a way for China to chart out new paths of influence but also as a necessity to compensate for the slow pace of domestic reforms. "China's leaders have, for all practical purposes, now conceded that a consumer-led growth strategy is tougher to pull off than originally thought," he says. "The consumption share of GDP has risen just 2.5 percentage points since 2010—far short of the boost to personal incomes that might be expected from the 7.5-percentage-point increase in the share of services and a 7.3-percentage-point increase in the high-wage urban share of its population over the same period." This disconnect, argues Roach, "reflects a porous social safety net that continues to foster high levels of fear-driven precautionary saving, which is inhibiting the growth of discretionary consumption. While still committed to urbanization and services development, China has elected to draw on a new external source of growth to compensate for a shortfall of internal demand."[44]

Singapore's former foreign minister George Yeo sees a positive outcome in China's new Silk Road in that he expects it to revitalize Southeast Asia.[45] Shaukat Aziz, the former prime minister of Pakistan, is also enthusiastic. "This will be a game-changer for

Pakistan," he says. "Linking up the Gwadar port with China through the rest of the country will vastly enhance our infrastructure. When roads, rail lines and telecom links are constructed they will open up whole areas of the country where there was little connection before to anything."[46]

Oxford University historian Peter Doimi de Frankopan puts China's initiative into historical context. "Precedents and parallels are important in providing intellectual credibility and framing the overarching vision of what is at stake," he writes, referring to the Belt and Road project. As Chinese president Xi Jinping said in Beijing in May 2017, the "ancient silk routes embody the spirit of peace and cooperation, openness and inclusiveness, mutual learning and mutual benefit." Frankopan goes on to compare China's initiative to the era of Pax Mongolica. "It is not surprising, of course, that the emphasis should be placed on the positive exchanges that were enabled and facilitated along the Silk Roads, rather than pointing out that disease, environmental change and violence also sometimes coursed along the arteries connecting east with west. Nevertheless, it is striking to note that while the rhythms along the Silk Roads were not always smooth, they compare favorably when set alongside those of Europe, whose history was shaped by almost never-ending confrontation and warfare."[47] For Frankopan, it is not an exaggeration to expect that "all roads will lead to Beijing" as Eurasia arises once again as the world economy's center of gravity.

The former governor of the Bank of India Raghuram Rajan is supportive of China's Silk Road project, but at the same time wary. "If the Belt and Road is part of a larger attempt to build out infrastructure it is good," he says. "Obviously, there is a certain degree of China centrism in this. But if the capabilities being built while building out this infrastructure allow for a further set of ties for development—logistical networks and citizen networks connecting different places—it can only help boost economic activity." However, Rajan warns, "the Chinese do have to be careful about the political implications of this project. It shouldn't be, and shouldn't be seen as, isolating certain groups or enabling certain countries at the expense of others. I'm not only talking about India, but globally. When one country pushes for a certain structure it is important to show inclusiveness and disinterestedness."[48] Indeed, in some quarters of South Asia, China's Belt and Road initiative is already being castigated as leading to "creditor imperialism."[49] Exhibit A in this charge is the Chinese-financed Hambantota port in Sri Lanka. When the debt proved unpayable by financially strapped Sri Lanka, the Chinese took it over.[50]

When Mohamad Mahathir returned to power in Malaysia in 2018, he promptly put China's major projects on hold, investigating corrupt kickbacks and disadvantageous terms negotiated by the previous government. Never one to hold his tongue, he also openly worried about "a new colonialism" fostered by China.[51] Similarly, the new Pakistani government elected in 2018 announced that it, too, would reconsider its projects with China because of the debt burden and unequal terms in the original agreements.

Clearly, China is a force to contend with as never before in the modern history of the West. How it governs itself and projects its power abroad will impact how the rest of us govern our own societies. Shaping globalization going forward will no longer be the sole province of the West but, of necessity, a joint endeavor with China. Both must figure out how to harness globalization so that it creates more winners than losers for its own people while cooperating as partners whenever convergent interests dictate.

POSITIVE NATIONALISM

Among the most pressing questions in the coming decades is whether globalization can ultimately be squared with the social trust that ensures belonging. In modern times, that trust has been registered in the nation-state and the communities within its borders. Is it possible, in the end, to balance sovereignty with the imperative of global cooperation in the face of challenges that transcend the capacities of nation-states to deal with on their own, such as climate change and pandemics, instability in financial flows, and open trading routes and communication networks? Can a global community of fate be established based on convergent interests among nations with distinct identities?

"Democracy, national sovereignty and global economic integration," Harvard's Dani Rodrik has famously argued, "are mutually incompatible: we can combine any two of the three, but never have all three simultaneously and in full." For Rodrik, globalization should be bent to fit the imperatives of democracy, not the other way around. "We need to rescue globalization not just from populists," he writes, "but also from its cheerleaders. Globalization evangelists have done great damage to their cause not just by underplaying the real fears and concerns on which the Trumps of this world thrive, but by overlooking the benefits of a more moderate form of globalization. We must reassess the balance between national autonomy and economic globalization. Simply put, we have pushed economic globalization too far—toward an impractical version that we might call 'hyper-globalization.'"[52]

Rodrik is right. The main pillars of the so-called neoliberal Washington Consensus behind hyperglobalization—free trade instead of fair trade, along with unregulated global capital flows, cuts in the safety net and in public investment aimed at compensatory adjustment for job losses in the most affected industries and regions—quite justifiably generated a backlash. Rodrik argues that, above all, "countries have the right to protect their institutional arrangements and safeguard the integrity of their regulations" and, in doing so, will chart diverse paths to prosperity. To make globalization work on the trade front, Rodrik calls for a return to a set of rules akin to the WTO's predecessor, the General Agreement on Tariffs and Trade. "It was a very thin and unambitious set of rules," says Rodrik, "and yet it worked extremely well. I think the secret to its success was that the old regime understood you need to provide countries with much greater policy space. A healthy international economy requires healthy domestic economies and policies."[53]

For Rodrik, there is no one-size-fits-all globalization. "I am in favor of allowing countries much greater latitude in the conduct of industrial policies," he argues. "When they succeed, this is good not only for the countries themselves but also for other nations because it enables economic growth and, hence, greater trade opportunities. When they fail, the costs are borne primarily by domestic consumers and taxpayers." For Rodrik, this includes the "Made in China 2025" project for dominance in high-tech, so disputed by the United States.[54]

Ernesto Zedillo, on the other hand, defends economic theorist David Ricardo and the philosophy of comparative advantage in trade. Blaming inequality and the squeeze of the middle class on trade, he argues, is a "deflection of responsibilities" by governing elites who have not done their job. "In principle," the former Mexican president says, the "three 'culprits' for increased inequality are acknowledged: technology, openness and policy—the TOP. But by suggesting that both skill-biased technological change and policies—such as taxation of capital and of highest incomes—happen to be endogenous to globalization, the latter ends up being the ultimate culprit. When this conclusion is accepted, then it becomes very tempting to proclaim that manipulation of the speed of globalization, including its reversion, could be an effective equalizing force." Furthermore, he argues, "the idea that policies—tax and otherwise—live inexorably in the straightjacket of globalization is also objectionable. Regressive tax policies, shrinking social safety nets, poor adjustment support, bad education and training policies, and crumbling infrastructure, among many others, are not inescapable consequences of globalization. They are explicit political choices, not inexorable outcomes of interdependence."[55]

Globalization has indeed worked for those countries that pursued such compensatory policies, mainly in Scandinavia. Through broad investment in common public goods such as infrastructure and education, much of Asia has fared well in the context of the global economy. "Globalization has not failed," says Singapore's Kishore Mahbubani.

> All discussions on globalization are distorted because Western analysts focus on the roughly 15 percent of the world's population who live in the West. They ignore the 85 percent who are the rest. The last 30 years of human history have been the best 30 years that the rest have enjoyed. Why? The answer is globalization. The rise of the middle class in Asia has spread wealth, faith in the possibility of fair international institutions and a stabilizing rules-based system that benefits the majority of humanity.... So why is there a perception that globalization has failed? The simple answer is that Western elites who enjoyed the fruits of globalization did not share them with their Western masses.[56]

Making globalization work for the West in the future thus means implementing policies of adjustment to ensure the benefits are shared instead of "deflecting responsibility," as through issuing jingoistic assertions of blame and closing one's country off from the world.

Former US treasury secretary Lawrence Summers has labeled this course "responsible nationalism." "A new approach has to begin from the idea that the basic responsibility of government is to maximize the welfare of its citizens," Summers said in an interview with us,

> not to pursue some abstract concept of the global good. Closely related to this is the idea that people want to feel that they are shaping the societies in which they live. It may be inevitable that impersonal forces of technology and changing global economic circumstances have profound effects. But it adds insult to injury when governments reach agreements that further cede control to international tribunals of one sort or another. This is especially the case when, for legal reasons or reasons of practicality, corporations have disproportionate influence in shaping global agreements.[57]

In a responsible nationalist approach, Summers has argued in a separate article, "the content of international agreements would be judged not by how much is harmonized or by how many barriers to global commerce are torn down but by whether people as workers, consumers and voters are empowered."[58] As an example, Summers cites how the protection of big-pharma companies' intellectual property rights has been prioritized in US international policy over shutting down tax havens, something that would actually benefit the average citizen, who is in effect paying the bill for corporate tax avoidance. He also argues for public investment in vocational training and public higher education as long-term adjustment strategies for coping with job displacement caused by both trade and technology change.

Making a similar point from another direction, Rana Foroohar argues that the bulk of employment and innovation in the United States is in small- and medium-sized privately held companies that invest more in their companies to improve productivity and expand employment than do large publicly held corporations. According to Foroohar, the evidence over the past twenty years suggests that more of the money companies kept through tax cuts aimed at repatriating capital from abroad ended up going into stock buybacks than into investment. Far more important to the small- and medium-sized firms—which source inputs largely from American supply chains—are more open immigration rules and tax credits for research and development. In short, creating jobs and boosting productivity are less about satisfying the profit imperatives of multinational companies than focusing on the needs of locally based private firms.[59]

Like Zedillo, Gordon Brown, the former British prime minister who led the G-20 nations away from the abyss of global depression after the financial crisis of 2008, argues against allowing nationalism to define the globalization narrative. Globalization was surely mismanaged, in his view, but the right narrative frame, as he told the authors, is to "accord nation-states as much autonomy as possible, but as much global cooperation as necessary." It is wrong-headed, he argued, to abide any nationalist narrative. "Policies exclusively focused on pulling the levers of the nation-state," he pointed out, "will fail to deal not just with pollution and inequality, but macroeconomic imbalances, beggar-thy-neighbor trade policies and their spillover effects, cyberattacks and pandemics—each of them [is a] transnational problem that requires an international response."

While conceding that nations will want to make their own tax decisions to suit local cultures and circumstances, Brown insists that failure to close down offshore tax havens will irretrievably damage any country's revenue base and its domestic plans for spending on education, health, and security. He further argues that "national governments must accept that they have an obligation to restrict excessive deficits and surpluses and prevent currency manipulation; but at the same time, macroeconomic imbalances can often best be limited by cooperative action, such as through the G-20."

As for global governance, Brown suggests "a worldwide early-warning system for financial markets, backed by globally applicable financial standards for capital, liquidity, transparency, and accountability." The former British prime minister's experience in the 2008–9 financial crisis taught him that a ceiling on debt creation in interconnected economies must be imposed when asset prices escalate too quickly, as they did during the housing bubble. Unless such monitoring is in place across all financial centers, "when the next crisis comes, we will still not know what is owned or owed by whom, where, and on what basis, and critics will ask why we have failed to learn the lessons from the financial contagion of 2008."

The kind of protectionist tariffs President Donald Trump imposed on some nations in 2018—including close allies Japan and Germany, as well as China—demonstrate precisely the wrong way to deal with the threats of globalization. He is right that China must shed the mercantilist aspects of its development strategy and open up markets more reciprocally. And it is certainly true that China's vast subsidization of solar power panels flooded the global market and put companies and their workers in the United States out of business. Yet a far better solution to disputes over aluminum or steel as well as new technology development, to take these as examples, would be to convene a global conference of producers to jointly curb overproduction until balance returns to the system, walling off the cascade of counterproductive consequences across the global economy. There is no reason a deal can't be negotiated with China just as a revamped NAFTA with Canada and Mexico was possible.

The challenge going forward is to avoid breaking the long peace of the past several decades that has been undergirded by the multilateral trading system while reassembling that system in response to present practices that have failed and to new changes that have taken place. By and large, this multilateral trade regime has succeeded in spreading prosperity, particularly to Asia—first to Japan and South Korea, then to China. Without question, those advances have come at the expense of certain industries and communities now politically awakened in the West, while benefiting other industries and communities. How to calculate and manage the deficits and benefits when value is added at each step along the line is now a complex exercise for which the blunt eighteenth-century instrument of national tariffs is a poor match.

Along with global expansion came an interdependence of supply chains in which end products for export consist of a mixed bag of imports from all over—for example, German cars manufactured in the United States for export to China, cars assembled in Mexico with US parts destined for export back to the United States, and iPhones engineered in the United States and assembled in China for export to the world. Indeed, foreign-invested enterprises were the source of 46 percent of total Chinese exports to the world in 2014; 60 percent of those shipments were bound for the United States.[60]

Further, the comparative advantages of trade in one integrated world have altered its composition as the once-advanced manufacturing powers have evolved into postindustrial societies in which services and information—from finance to entertainment to digital networks—make up the bulk of economic activity and exports. The United States has a large trade surplus with the world in those areas.[61]

Keeping the long peace amidst so much change will be possible only if all players settle, in the end, on an inclusive rule-based order that governs their interactions. As former WTO head Pascal Lamy has pointed out insightfully, such an order suited to the rapidly evolving economies of the twenty-first century has to fit the reality of "one world, three systems." As he puts it, the US system is hyper-capitalist, individualistic, and entrepreneurial; China is a strong collectivist state mixed with robust market competition; Europe and many others are somewhere in between. As former Italian Prime Minister Mario Monti once put it pithily, Europe's social market system must be able to coexist and interact fairly with China's socialist market economy. By definition, unilateral action that seeks advantage over mutual benefit in a deeply interdependent system threatens the order upon which peace rests. History has demonstrated that whenever economic war erupts, dire consequences are never far behind.

Only such a rules-based system can make globalization a win-win prospect for all involved. As former US president Bill Clinton argued in an interview with the authors, building up one's own country in the ways suggested here—what he calls "positive nationalism"—does not contradict the imperative of global cooperation. It is the precondition for it.

OPEN SOCIETIES' NEED FOR DEFINED BORDERS

If real or perceived economic dislocation from hyperglobalization has been one key driver of the anti-establishment, nationalist, and nativist backlash, immigration has been the other.

Any new social contract that spreads the wealth of the Digital Age more inclusively must be adopted through deliberative consent of the governed within the jurisdiction of the nation-state and its communities, since the nation-state remains the primary locus of democratic legitimacy. Unless the governed consider that social contract to be a fair balance of benefits and burdens shared by all, it won't hold. Societies and cultures are not closed systems, but the capacities of the welfare and public investment state are bound by the fiscal realities of territories with boundaries. For that reason, nation-states have the right to control immigration based on criteria that ensure newcomers will not only abide by the values and norms of the host nation but also be able to contribute positively to a given jurisdiction's economy and tax base and not be a drain on finite resources. These two issues—how immigrants from other cultures and religions fit into the host nations on whose shores they have arrived, and how they are integrated into that nation's economic life and social welfare arrangements—have become front-and-center concerns in a world of greater human flows than ever before.

Samuel Huntington, author of the famous "clash of civilizations" thesis, put his finger on the other flash point of global cultural politics. "The immigration issue," he wrote presciently in 2004, "may produce serious divisions among elites groups, arouse popular opinion against immigrants and immigration, and offer opportunities to nationalist and populist politicians and parties to exploit these sentiments."[62] As we are reminded nearly every week when boatloads of refugees are rescued from drowning in the Mediterranean on their way to Europe, the oldest and most rapidly shrinking population of Europe sits astride the most youthful and rapidly growing population of Africa, which the United Nations estimates will host 4 billion people by 2100.[63]

Huntington was quite right on this score. That the most liberal societies on the planet are facing a crisis of intolerance over refugees and immigration should give us pause for reflection. It would be wrong to simply condemn all those who cherish and want to protect the "communities of fate" in which they are vested as somehow seeking to resurrect the ghost of Hitler. While defending openness, diversity, and tolerance as core principles, we should be careful not to blithely ascribe racist or xenophobic motives to a defense of belonging. It is, after all, what we have historically meant by cultural pluralism in the West; it should not be conflated with aggressive nationalism.

During the Cold War years, nationalist sentiment was mostly frozen in the ice blocs of ideological competition. Unfettered nationalism, still closely associated with the horrors of World War II, was widely held to be taboo. As French president Francois Mitterrand, one of the architects of the historic European project to curb sovereign rivalries through greater integration, famously put it, "Nationalism means war."

Pluralism: From the Defense of Culture to Tolerance of the Other

When the Soviet bloc collapsed and the Cold War thawed, the hot passions of nationalism reemerged. Its first post–Cold War outburst, in the early 1990s, took the form of the Balkan Wars, which pitted ethnic groups against one another in the dismantled

Yugoslavia. During that conflict, in 1991, one of the authors sat down with the great pluralist philosopher Isaiah Berlin to discuss this renewed phenomenon in a seaside café in Portofino, Italy, where the Oxford don spent his summers. Then nearly ninety, Berlin, who was born in Latvia, was widely admired for such seminal works as "Two Concepts of Liberty" and "The Hedgehog and the Fox." They became foundational texts of liberal thought.

In our conversation on the Italian coast, Berlin sought to distinguish between aggressive and nonaggressive nationalism. In his view, aggressive nationalism, such as what he had witnessed in Hitler's Germany and we see today in Vladimir Putin's Russia, resulted from a reaction against humiliation, "like a bent twig, forced down so severely that when released, it lashes back with fury," as he put it.

Nonaggressive nationalism, on the other hand, was not animated by humiliation. And it was not about ethnic purity or sacred soil. It was about belonging to a unique and incommensurate way of life among one's own kind, a particular *Volksgeist*, or community of fate that shared a language, common memories, and customs. In formulating this definition, Berlin was influenced by the eighteenth-century German romantic thinker Johann Gottfried Herder. For Herder, the "villains of history" were the great conquerors such as Alexander the Great, Caesar, and Charlemagne and the universalists of the French Enlightenment "who stomped out native cultures." From his own day, Berlin would add Hollywood-inspired mass culture as a culprit. "Herder virtually invented the idea of belonging," Berlin said. "He believed that just as people need to eat and drink, to have security and freedom of movement, so too they need to belong to a group. Deprived of this, they feel cut off, lonely, diminished, unhappy.... To be human means to be able to feel at home somewhere, with your own kind."[64]

For Berlin, as for Herder, only what was unique had true value. Cosmopolitanism in their view was an empty vessel. "To be human means to belong," Berlin argued. "If the streams dry up ... where men and women are not products of a culture, where they don't have kith and kin and feel closer to some people than to others, where there is no native language—that would lead to a tremendous desiccation of everything that is human."

The borders that came down after the end of the Cold War were further weakened by efforts at integration that entailed the freer flow of people. Immigrants, legal and illegal, entering the core of Europe were seeking a better life that promised rising prosperity. By definition, mass immigration challenges Berlin's definition of cultural pluralism. By the early years of the twenty-first century, it had come to mean something quite different: tolerance for the culture of incoming migrants, rather than preservation of a way of life distinct from that of others. But if belonging to a unique way of life among kith and kin with common memories is what it means to be human, as Berlin says, how can these two ideas of cultural pluralism be reconciled? This question of identity is at the heart of the clash between nativist populism and globalizing liberal culture that has erupted in the heart of the modernizing West.

From a different angle, Pankaj Mishra, the Indian author of *The Age of Anger*, traces the course of this clash from its origins outside the West during the age of imperialism and US dominance to its arrival in Berlin and London today. After preparing for a civil service career in Indian universities, this maverick Che Guevara–look-alike scholar changed course and retreated for five years to read and write books on subjects from butter chicken to Buddhism in the tiny Himalayan hamlet of Mashobra. From that vantage point, he developed strong views about the decimation of local cultures by globalization.

This present-day Herder argues that "naïve people, the free-marketeers and globalizers, did not know what they were doing—that they were dismantling a whole system of interlocking and necessary fictions that societies and individuals have needed since the death of God to give a degree of meaning, purpose and stability to their lives."[65] In Mishra's view, the broad disaffection with homogenizing universalism he has witnessed around the developing world has now spread to large constituencies in the West. "They too now see a threat to their way of life and belonging posed by distant and faceless elites," he writes. "Their mutiny against the system that has produced this outcome is the motivating force behind the current populist wave. For these disrupted communities, the promises of globalization haven't panned out. Their jobs disappeared. Their communities lost any sense of internal affinity. To take back control of their fate, they embraced Brexit or Trump or became followers of Le Pen."

Elif Shafak, the prolific Turkish novelist who divides her time between London and Istanbul, tries to square the circle. "An absolute universalism was problematic in the way in which it erased cultural, ethnic, linguistic diversity," she said in an interview. "The opposite, cultural relativism, was also problematic." Her third way between these historically spent alternatives is what she calls "progressive humanism." For Shafak, this middle way "is a system of thought that gives prime importance not to ethnicity or race, sex, class or religion, but to human beings per se. It is a way of connecting with fellow human beings across boundaries by both recognizing diversity, plurality and differences, and at the same time insisting on shared universal values and the need for coexistence." Getting the balance right, she goes on, means "we cannot leave patriotism to the nationalists ... and we cannot leave emotions to populist demagogues."[66] Shafak's thinking closely parallels that of the philosopher Kwame Anthony Appiah, who chairs the Berggruen Philosophy Prize jury. As Appiah argues in his 2018 book, *The Lies That Bind,* we should all wear our identities "lightly" since we are all, in effect, mongrels descended from mixed circumstances in our personal histories.[67]

Ethical Universalism

But how can that balance be achieved in actual practice?

Slavoj Žižek, the Slovenian philosopher, is the provocative bad boy of this debate. Žižek is irritated both by the liberal demonization of anyone who thinks their culture is worth protecting against newcomers and by the "tolerant" paternalism of cosmopolitan elites who turn a blind eye to practices of some Muslim immigrants such as arranging marriages, brutalizing gays, and preventing their children from going to state schools. In a nod to Herder and Berlin, he argues that "one of the great Left taboos will have to be broken here: the notion that the protection of one's specific way of life is in itself a proto-Fascist or racist category. If we don't abandon this notion, we open up the way for the anti-immigrant wave which thrives all around Europe."[68] To frustrate that wave, Žižek, like Shafak, insists that a defense of one's own way of life does not exclude "ethical universalism" practiced by both immigrants and host cultures.

We had better get used to this dual way of thinking, he says, echoing Huntington, because we now live in a world in which large nomadic migrations are part of the "plastic" future that globalization has wrought. Refugees and immigrants, as he puts it, "are the price of a global economy." Here is how Žižek defines what Pope Francis has called "reconciled diversity" in this new world:

No tolerance of religious, sexist or ethnic violence on any side, no right to impose onto others one's own way of life or religion, respect of every individual's freedom to abandon his/her communal customs. If a woman chooses to cover her face, her choice should be respected, but if she chooses not to cover it, her freedom to do so has to be guaranteed. Yes, such a set of rules privileges the Western European way of life, but it is a price for European hospitality.[69]

The Canadian philosopher Charles Taylor, who was awarded the Berggruen Prize for Philosophy in 2016,[70] has offered perhaps the most salient approach to establishing a modus vivendi in a diverse and mobile planet. It is the eighty-six-year-old philosopher's thinking about the recognition of irreducible diversity in an interdependent world of plural identities—and how societies can cope with this reality—that gives his ideas urgent relevance in this era of Trump, Brexit, the burkini ban, and the rise of the anti-immigrant right.

Reasonable Accommodation

Taylor's approach does not deny clashes of cultures, whether French-speaking Quebecois in his native Canada or pious Muslims in predominantly secular Europe. Rather it acknowledges the frictions head-on through what he calls "a language of perspicuous contrast," or the clearly expressed delineation of differences as the basis for reconciliation and "reasonable accommodation" of each to the other(s). This intercultural undertaking contrasts sharply with multicultural identity silos that foster separation, hostility, and resentment instead of integration. "To have this bland neo-liberal view that there are no major cultural contradictions at all, and things will all go swimmingly, that we'll all just globalize … this is the absolute nadir of blindness,"

Taylor has said.[71] "We want to get these differences out into a sphere where there can be a rational and calm discussion of how to live together with tension between different groups. It's only by coming to such a language that we can have a discussion that doesn't degenerate into a kind of stigmatizing of the other.... We need it very badly in our diverse societies." For Taylor, language that evolves to express and absorb new experience—including the presence of strangers entering into vernacular ways of life—is itself the enframing tool of human diversity.

Taylor walks the talk. He led the effort to keep Quebec as part of Canada through recognition of its distinctive character in a key 1995 referendum.[72] More recently, he cochaired a commission appointed by the provincial government of Quebec to explore how to accommodate mostly new Muslim immigrants.[73] That difficult discourse is still going on, and is far from settled. In 2017 the conservative provincial government in Quebec banned Islamic dress that covers women's faces. Nevertheless, as a result of Taylor's public stances, followed up by Prime Minister Justin Trudeau in practice, Canada is seen worldwide as a model of both integration and tolerance.

What is not often known about Canada's success with immigrants, however, is the restrictive nature of its policies. Although Canada took in 25,000 Syrian refugees in 2015–16 in response to the horrific civil war, it otherwise has a rigorous merit-based point system that prioritizes incoming financial resources and immigrant skills that match the needs of the labor market over preference for family or relatives. As Harvard University's Paul May has noted, "In the US, about two-thirds of permanent residents are admitted to reunite with family members. Less than 20 percent are admitted because of their professional skills. In Canada, by contrast, it's almost the opposite: more than 60 percent of permanent residents are admitted via the economy class, and only a quarter are admitted because of family reunification."[74]

During the immigration debate in the United States in 2017, President Donald Trump was excoriated by the media for saying he didn't want the United States to become like Sweden with a large, unintegrated immigrant community. But Trump was not wrong. Aje Carlbom, an anthropologist at Malmo University, describes his country's problem: "Sweden is statistically one of the worst countries at integration of foreigners. Why? Mainly because this is a highly complex country where you can't get a job without education. Many of those who come are uneducated." The statistics bear him out. In both Sweden and neighboring Norway, foreigners are three times more likely to be unemployed than locals.[75] In short, it is education, not immigration status, that determines who gets a job.

Even in these advanced countries with a reputation for humanitarian policies, open arms to immigrants uncoordinated with economic need can disrupt the very governing model that made them so successful when their societies were largely homogenous. Political scientist Fabrizio Tassinari has been one of the few to emphasize that the Nordic countries' success has been largely due to an "efficient and impartial technocracy" with "bureaucratic autonomy" that people trust because it keeps politics out of administration and delivers the goods inclusively. But that trust, he says, has been founded on a "watertight social contract" between citizens and the state that is now fraying. As large immigrant groups enter the picture, all do not assume the same norms and obligations with their rights, and they are inevitably suspected as taking from society but not contributing to it. "The upheavals and wide divergence among Scandinavia countries in their responses to Europe's refugee crisis testify to the risk," Tassinari has written.[76] Norway's prime minister Erna Solberg makes the same point from another angle. "When you are a country that is well off with a generous welfare system … you become the most attractive destination" for immigrants, she warns.[77]

Mix and Move On

Finding the right balance will involve a continuing discourse within democracies. Former president Bill Clinton lays out a moral and historical frame for the United States, in particular, that keeps future immigration policy choices in perspective. "We know from the human genome that all people are 99.5 percent the same," he argued to the authors in an interview. "Some people seem to spend 99 percent of their time worrying about the 0.5 percent that is different. That is a big mistake. We should focus on what we have in common. We make better decisions in diverse societies than in homogenous ones. America's great advantage is that we are an idea, not a place. We are not an ethnicity or a uniform culture. Those who promote this nativist view are playing Russian roulette with our biggest ticket to the future."[78]

"Even if you believe we are headed to the first big change since the industrial revolution with robots and digital technology that will kill more jobs than it creates, we are still going to need diversity," says Clinton. "We are going to need creative cooperation. To do that, we need some fair back-and-forth with others not like us. Resentment-based divisive politics is a mistake. This is just the latest chapter in the oldest drama of human history— us versus them. But sooner or later we mix and move on."[79]

The only alternative to "reasonably accommodating" each other is a return to the "barbarism" of a clash of civilizations. But avoiding a backlash that invites this nativism entails aligning the humanitarian impulse with the economic realities of host countries. Bad faith results from good intentions if the capacity to fulfill moral claims is lacking. To ignore this dimension in any country undermines the social contract that is the foundation of effective governance.

ONE WORLD, MANY SYSTEMS

As national sovereignty reasserts itself and one size of globalization does not fit all, one world with many systems will characterize the international order in the decades ahead. A new modus vivendi that accepts this reality must be found among different cultures and civilizations now tied together as never before in a web of mutual dependence—a web in which the weight of the global economy has shifted from the once-regnant developed world to the emerging economies.[80]

For this evolution to unfold with a modicum of stability, the success or failure of diverse models of governance that arise out of plural civilizational and cultural contexts must rest on competition over results, not on the dogma of a dominant ideology, interference by others, or imposition by force—in short, a global system of "diverse equilibrium" in which the power of example, not the example of power, prevails. That is what globalization in which "one size does not fit all" will look like.

Paradoxically, Donald Trump's "America First" posture may turn out to be the midwife of such a new equilibrium. By rejecting the Paris Climate Accord, pulling out of trade agreements, parting ways with the United States' European allies, and shirking the country's long-standing liberal internationalism, he is paving the way for an alternative order in which the United States as a nation-state is no longer the dominant player. By default, those who move in to fill the vacuum will determine the new balance of power. By withdrawing from a leadership role in shaping globalization, the United States doesn't stop the process; it only opens the path for the rise of new players.

On climate change, for example, we have already seen in response the emergence of a "network of the willing"—ranging from China and the European Union to subnational entities like the state of California—to carry on global cooperation. Through Governor Jerry Brown's leadership, 188 subnational entities in 39 countries on 6 continents are pushing ahead to implement the Paris Climate Accord despite its abandonment by official Washington. Former World Trade Organization chief Pascal Lamy even talks of a "plurilateral" world order of nongovernmental organizations, businesses, and subnational entities instead of a "multilateral" order based on nation-states.

While all nations and networks must have their respected place in any globally inclusive arrangement, in the end the key pillars of such an order, in which the management of convergent interests is bound by commonly agreed rules, must be the United States and China—the world's two largest economies, which also represent highly distinct civilizational spheres. For globalization to work, it needs leadership. Yet, as the late Zbigniew Brzezinski pointed out, neither the United States nor China can lead on its own. American power has diminished, and China is not yet ready or able to step up to the plate, and may never be prepared to take on the role.[81]

If both fail to buy in as indispensable partners, such an order can't take hold globally. The urgent concern is that these two giants are headed in opposite directions. As former Australian prime minister Kevin Rudd has eloquently put it, "In the absence of a common narrative shared by the United States and

China, the two nations are likely to drift more rapidly apart. Trust builds on itself just as distrust builds on itself as well, compounding into deep enmity over time."[82] Time is short, and distrust is building.

The alternative to a world order anchored in a partnership of its two most influential nations looks grim. Alongside the new networks of the willing, swaths of pandemonium fostered by the unwilling will likely then surround gated outposts that are linked to one another but divorced from their planetary hinterland in a kind of global apartheid system.

A new dark age could descend in some regions where tyrants abuse their subjects and where jihadists or criminal gangs roam freely to terrorize dispossessed populations. That so much of this sounds familiar—the brutal carnage of the Syrian civil war being the most tragic case in point—is a frightening indication of just how real the peril is. And, as we have further seen in the enduring refugee crisis and wave of mass migration, those who can flee will seek to breach the gates in search of a better life on the other side. In many ways, this is the price of leaderless globalization left to its own dynamics without effective cooperation or governing institutions.

At the height of the Syrian refugee crisis in 2015, Antonio Guterres, then the United Nations high commissioner for refugees and now the UN secretary general, warned that such a world was already in the making: "We live in a period in which we no longer have a unipolar or bipolar world. We don't even have a multipolar world; it's kind of a chaotic world where power relations have become unclear. When power relations are unclear, impunity and unpredictability tend to prosper. That, I believe, is the reality behind the high levels of displacement that are taking place in today's world."[83]

But partnership between the United States and China is far easier said than done. Unlike the transatlantic order now receding, which was bound together at its core by common cultural and political foundations, the United States and China come from very different civilizational roots. The Middle Kingdom has historically defined itself by its centrality and uniqueness in the world going back millennia; the United States' comparatively young identity is associated with universality and the mission of spreading its values. China's geopolitical model has always been that of a dominant power surrounded by tributaries. By contrast, the United States, following the experience of Europe after the Treaty of Westphalia gave birth to the nation-state, has managed its international relations by seeking a global balance of power among states. A "cross-civilizational" partnership between these two traditions is unprecedented.

With respect to China's role in its own region, Henry Kissinger's formula is the most realistic arrangement for the next twenty years. "It's understandable that China wants to keep foreigners from approaching its borders and it therefore undertakes a defense effort to that end," he says. "I particularly understand it in light of China's history. It's also understandable that the United States doesn't want any region dominated by a superpower, so that creates a certain balance. The two elements in that balance, namely China and the United States, also have to lead in cooperation."[84] Kissinger has rightly come to understand that, in today's linked world, we need a fresh approach: partnership must become an integral part of the balance of power in any new geopolitical arrangement.[85] The danger of war looms most menacingly if the balance of power is reduced to only a military dimension. With no common intent on any front, all else will dwell in the dark shadow of distrust in which each will seek advantage over the other.

For a US-China partnership to work, as Fu Ying once told Kissinger, the United States must be able to accept China as "an equal brother."[86] But that goes both ways: China must also step up with a global perspective on its responsibility that it has never before held—not as an honorary member of the Western club, but as coarchitect of world order. This recognition is the cornerstone of a strategy of evolutionary stability that aims to avoid a power vacuum by maintaining order over the slow course of change.

The cause of war and conflict historically has not only been a clash between established and rising powers over who is top dog. It has also resulted from the gap that emerges in the provision of "global public goods" when the old power that provided them diminishes without a new power or set of powers stepping into the breach.

The Xi-Obama deal on curbing climate change announced at the Asia-Pacific Economic Cooperation (APEC) Summit in November 2014 was a welcome, even historic step, consolidated later in the Paris Accord, in the direction of a partnership for providing a global public good. In the Obama era, China and the United States also partnered on the two most significant challenges to nuclear nonproliferation—North Korea and Iran.

There has also been tentative US-China cooperation in a range of other areas, such as cyber security. where, for the first time, during Xi's state visit while Obama was president, China and the United States started down the long road of cyber-détente by agreeing to the basic principle of not attacking each other's vital infrastructure. Along with differences over freedom of expression on the internet and technological advances, cyberspying and cyberwar are the issues most likely to drive a wedge between the two nations.

Although urgent realism has led President Trump to seek a partnership between the United States and China on North Korea, his embrace of a fossil fuel future for America and his withdrawal from the Paris climate treaty and the Iran nuclear accord rolled back the Obama level of cooperation. Since all other nations remain in the Paris Accord, it is likely only a matter of time and the cascading effects of climate change before the United States inevitably returns to the fold in the post-Trump era. It remains to be seen whether reality will ultimately also force a return to negotiation and cooperation on trade issues and some form of the Iran accord, either during the late years of the Trump term or after.

Clearly, no mileage is to be gained in being naïve on either side. As China resumes its role as the dominant regional power for no other reason than being the biggest economy around, it will ipso facto challenge the leading role of the United States in the East Asia alliance system that has Japan at its core, drawing surrounding neighbors into its orbit. We've already seen the weaning away of Philippine allegiance to the US alliance, with President Duterte even blurting out, "Bye-bye America" at one point.[87]

To date the US-dominated security arrangement has maintained stability by providing a defense umbrella for Japan—against North Korea as well as China—so that it has had no incentive to remilitarize. If that umbrella were to fold, Japan would inevitably bolster its own military capabilities—including the addition of nuclear weapons. The big question for the intermediate future is whether the United States will remain as a balancer in the region or if Japan, cut loose from American protection, and China can be counted on to restrain themselves. The optimum alternative would involve both countries, along with the United States, joining in a common pact that ensures freedom of navigation and security against outside threats or military imbalances within the region.

In the end, the best hope of avoiding the Thucydides trap of a clash between a rising and an established power with its alliances is to imbed Japan and China, along with the Korean Peninsula, in a common institutional framework that diminishes tensions—not unlike historic enemies France and Germany did in Europe after World War II. A resolution of the North Korea crisis that results in a formal peace treaty and some level of nuclear disarmament verified by Chinese-led inspectors, more trusted by Pyongyang than Westerners, could provide the embryo of such a regionally inclusive security framework.

As difficult as it may be for the United States to share leadership in the Asia-Pacific region that it has dominated for decades, it will also be a big concession for China to embrace the notion of a balance of power instead of a series of tributaries. In the end, where differences remain, the two nations must ensure their mutual interests by accommodating each other with these principles of security: restraint in the use of power, reciprocity in actions taken, transparency over intentions, and sufficient capabilities and resilience to assure the ability to strike back and restore equilibrium if attacked.[88]

The new global order we envision on the basis of the United States and China as indispensable partners would accommodate the return of diversity from a long interlude of hegemony—for the first time in history "diversity connected in real time"—and would be structured geopolitically as "one world, many systems." This new rules-based system would be a kind of "Westphalia plus" in which partnerships on global issues of concern to all form a *constituent part* of the balance of power between and among states—in other words, a system in which trust-building cooperative arrangements and institutions are not an alternative but themselves a factor in the overall configuration of power.[89]

To stabilize world order on these terms, the United States and China must serve as guarantors of global public goods—open trade and investment, stable financial flows, climate protection, freedom of travel and navigation, sharing of health knowledge and scientific advances. The cornerstone of a "non-value-based" partnership founded on convergent interests will inevitably have to coexist with "value-based plurilateralism" among the like-minded. Its role would be to mobilize joint efforts of those whose values are aligned in the pursuit of common ends without resort to the use of force or organized subversion against others—with the exception of the most egregious humanitarian violations by a state or organized groups within a state. When values conflict, "taking a stand, not taking sides" would be the modus operandi.

In a world of more equal powers, imperialism, intervention, and "nation-building others' nations" are anachronisms and, in any case, counterproductive.

Policies of engagement and transparency create a sense of security while nativism, isolation, and censorship breed suspicion and misapprehension. Sharing of the same information about what is really going on may well not forge agreement among all participants, but it does invite human understanding. To dwell in darkness and ignorance about the other's motives and intentions subjects events to the "power of the wrong metaphor"—"This is like Munich" or "This is like the Cold War," for example—and such comparisons all too easily invite conflict. When fear of others is diminished, on the other hand, horizons widen and cultures are more welcoming to outside influences. This leads to a positive-sum ecosystem that draws on distinct models of governance, each further perfected through competition with others.

Only within such a stable framework will societies feel secure enough to open up, recognize common interests, and pursue cooperation. Scientific and technological advances can then be shared by all, and diverse cultures can flourish simultaneously, enriched by the cross-pollination of a new global civilization in the making.

Our Image of the Future Shapes the Present

What we seek to do above all in this book is to avoid the usual proposals that lack imagination by positing old solutions to new problems. We have also tried to show that, in this age of disruption, there is no final fix to a problem or a definitive end point, but only continuous renovation that adapts to ever-evolving circumstances. As Chinese wisdom has long understood, solving one problem creates the next. The aim of governance is to balance stability and change—what we call "evolutionary stability"—so that the stride and scope of social transformation can be absorbed by our incremental natures. The long march to adapt society's institutions to new conditions is preferable to abrupt breaks that create vacuums of authority with no governing narrative. Such a vacuum is the breeding space for the wishful thinking, intolerance, and even violence that often accompanies populism.

With respect to the renovation of democracy, we offer a way to think about the structural redesign of governing institutions instead of tweaking the edges of the present system and looking to the restoration of "our" partisans in the halls of power. We propose integrating the participatory power of social networks and direct democracy with representative government by creating new, nonpartisan mediating bodies—participation without populism—that restore the kind of deliberative ballast to popular sovereignty envisioned by America's Founders as the essential safeguard of enduring republics.

Fundamental and enduring change can most realistically start from the bottom, where people are much closer to government, and advance upward. In the United States historically, all significant institutional innovation has come from the states.

We also argue that the business model of the social media giants that prioritizes virality over the spread of truthful and trustworthy information subverts democracy rooted in informed consent of the voting public. Here, too, checks and balances must be established so that democratic discourse is dispassionately guided by objective observation and verified fact.

To take on the challenge of precarious employment in the Digital Age, this era of steady disruption through innovation, we propose a universal safety net that protects workers, not specific jobs—flexicurity. To address inequality, we look beyond the industrial-era panacea of income redistribution to new ways to share wealth by providing all with an equity stake in owning the robots—"universal basic capital," instead of a basic income—and widely fostering opportunity by bolstering the ladder of upward mobility. We call these predistribution policies. Certainly, fairness dictates progressive, redistributive taxation, but the fundamental response to growing inequality in market economies is to increase the predistribution wealth of the small saver and spread digital-era skills through investment in public higher education and infrastructure—all of which disproportionately benefit the less well-off.

Globalization is the inexorable outcome of open systems linked by modern-day commerce, communication, technology, and transportation. The cross-pollination of cultures and civilizations it fosters enriches humanity as a whole. If ungoverned and leaderless, however, it can create more losers than winners.

To harness globalization, we argue, nation-states and communities must ensure fairness and reciprocity in trade, curb tax avoidance by multinational companies, and coordinate macroeconomic policies so that asset bubbles and global financial flows don't wreak havoc through contagion across interconnected economic systems. Tax, regulatory, and social policies that compensate and adjust for the dislocations of an open trading system must be established through legitimate processes of democratic deliberation within each country and not be subject to the dictates of distant technocratic bodies. All can prosper from the comparative advantages of trade—if governing elites avoid "deflecting responsibility" and instead put in place the proper domestic safety nets and opportunity webs for their population that ensure those advantages are shared. At the same time, the systemic links of interdependence created by recent decades of globalization require coordination and cooperation at the global level where national interests converge or where addressing common challenges—such as climate change—are beyond the capacity of national action. "Positive nationalism" that tends primarily to the welfare of a country's own citizens is not antithetical to global cooperation; it is the precondition for it.

Jurisdictions bound by fiscal realities have the right to control immigration across their borders, we argue, so that the social contract that binds national belonging is not undermined or swamped. Successful integration entails matching the skills and education levels of immigrants with the needs of the host economy. While we embrace the value of diversity in open societies, we argue that "reasonable accommodation," each to the other, of newcomers and host cultures must bend toward the latter while adhering to the ethical universality of personal dignity and gender equality.

Reasonable accommodation to each other—instead of falling into the trap in which rising and established powers inevitably head toward conflict and war—also characterizes our approach to a new balance between the West and China.

Now that China has risen to the top ranks of the global economy by taking advantage of US-led globalization, the knee-jerk response is to treat it as a Cold War–type rival, even an enemy to be contained. We call instead for building a partnership around convergent interests—climate change, nuclear nonproliferation, global financial stability, open but fair trade—as an integral part of the balance of power, instead of once again lapsing into a dangerous world divided into geopolitical blocs and spheres of influence.

To keep the peace, a balance of power among strategic rivals is a wise objective for any nation. But unless partnership on matters of mutual interest are in the mix of calculating that balance, a metric of military might alone tends to risk war—each side will seek advantage over the other in the name of defense. If there is no sense of common intent on any front, all else dwells in the dark shadow of distrust.

The ascendant leaders of the twenty-first century have not so much spelled out policies as offered a vision for how the disillusioned, disenchanted, and disenfranchised can once again take control of their lives. Populist leaders like Donald Trump, Vladimir Putin, and Hungary's Viktor Orban assert a posture of grievance planted in an ideal past. In contrast to this xenophobic and closed-society approach, youthful leaders like Canada's Justin Trudeau and France's Emmanuel Macron promote an aspirational politics rooted in a complex future. However they may stumble politically during their tenure, this latter sort of leader is on the right track. They embrace a politics of openness, inclusivity, diversity, innovation, and sustainability as the core strengths of a society and the path to renovation.

In China, President Xi Jinping fits neither mold neatly. He, too, is a culturally conservative strongman. But he sees himself more as the present custodian of an ancient civilization that he seeks to revitalize than as a leader yearning for an ideal past. How the rejuvenation of China's legacy articulates with the interests of others—for example, through the "new phase of globalization" Xi is promoting by revitalizing the old Silk Road trading routes in an effort to tie together commerce and culture from Beijing through Eurasia to Africa—is a central concern going forward. Whether this is good or bad for the rest of the world—a "win-win" strategy as Xi likes to put it—will depend on the extent to which China can enhance the interests of others along with its own.

It is the outcome of this contest of contrasting visions, this framing of choices about what future we want, that will determine whether the world comes together instead of falls apart.

To take hold, any vision with a chance of enduring realization must give people and nations alike confidence that they are once again in charge of their destiny, that they have as fair a shot as anyone else in making something of their lives. The Nobel scientist Ilya Prigogine understood that the present doesn't determine the future so much as our image of the future determines what we do in the present. Following this insight, to succeed at renovating our societies today, we must paint a convincing image of a future in which everyone has a place.[1]

NOTES

PREFACE

1. Our first book on the subject, *Intelligent Governance for the 21st Century: A Middle Way between West and East* (New York: Polity Press, 2015), was designated a book of the year by the *Financial Times*.

2. Dale Kasler, "California the World's Fifth Largest Economy? Look Out, Britain," *Sacramento Bee,* July 16, 2017, http://www.sacbee.com/news/politics-government/capitol-alert/article161472333.html.

CHAPTER 1

1. Francis Fukuyama, "The Emergence of a Post-fact World," *LiveMint,* December 30, 2016, http://www.livemint.com/Opinion/93hZcSFMVKtz4y5cTylOxI/Francis-Fukuyama—The-emergence-of-a-postfact-world.html.

2. Nathan Gardels, "The Biological Origins of Culture: An Interview with Antonio Damasio," *The WorldPost,* February 28, 2018, https://www.washingtonpost.com/news/theworldpost/wp/2018/02/28/culture/?utm_term=.c71f54b07dao.

3. Gates letter in the Bill and Melinda Gates Foundation Annual Report, January 2015.

4. Stefano Rellandini, "Pope Says World's Many Conflicts Amount to Piecemeal World War Three," Reuters, September 13, 2014, https://www.reuters.com/article/us-pope-war/pope-says-worlds-many-conflicts-amount-to-piecemeal-world-war-three-idUSKBN0H808 L20140913.

5. Walter Russell Mead, "Have We Gone from a Post-war to a Pre-war World?" *The WorldPost,* July 07, 2017, http://www.huffingtonpost.com/walter-russell-mead/new-global-war_b_5562664.html.

6. Nathan Gardels, "How to Be Alone in Our Techno-consumer Culture: A Conversation with Jonathan Franzen," *The WorldPost,* January 30, 2014, http://www.huffingtonpost.com/2014/01/27/jonathan-franzen-consumer-culture_n_4677753.html

7. Orhan Pamuk, *A Strangeness in My Mind* (New York: Alfred A. Knopf, 2015).

8. Amartya Sen, *Identity and Violence* (New York: W.W. Norton, 2007).

9. Niall Ferguson *The Square and the Tower* (New York: Penguin Press, 2018), 83–85.

10. Carl Schmitt, *Concept of the Political* (Chicago: University of Chicago Press, 1995).

11. Noah Bierman, "Trump's Popularity at CPAC Gathering, Which He Shunned a Year Ago, Shows How He's Conquered Conservatives," *Los Angeles Times,* February 24, 2017, http://www.latimes.com/politics/la-na-pol-trump-cpac-20170224-story.html.

12. Max Bearak, "Theresa May Criticized the Term 'Citizen of the World'. But Half the World Identifies That Way," *Washington Post,* October 05, 2016, https://www.washingtonpost.com/news/worldviews/wp/2016/10/05/theresa-may-criticized-the-term-citizen-of-the-world-but-half-the-world-identifies-that-way/?utm_term=.5acbc8f3c338.

13. David Goodhart, *The Road to Somewhere: The Populist Revolt and the Future of Politics* (London: C. Hurst, 2017).

14. Javier Solana and Strobe Talbott, "The Decline of the West, and How to Stop It," *New York Times,* October 19, 2016, https://www.nytimes.com/2016/10/20/opinion/the-decline-of-the-west-and-how-to-stop-it.html.

15. Nathan Gardels, "Weekend Roundup: Macron's Challenge Has Global Resonance," *The WorldPost,* May 12, 2017, http://www.huffingtonpost.com/entry/weekend-roundup-169_us_59149cdae4b030d 4f1fod6bd.

16. Regis Debray, "God and the Political Planet," in "Islam in the 21st Century," special issue, *New Perspectives Quarterly* 25, no. 4 (Fall 2008): 115–19, http://www.digitalnpq.org/archive/2002_winter/debray.html.

17. Interview with Regis Debray, "The Third World: From Kalashnikovs to God and Computers," *New Perspectives Quarterly* 3, no. 1 (Spring 1986): 25–28, http://www.digitalnpq.org/archive/1986_spring /kalashnikov.html.

18. Regis Debray, "Eloge des Frontières," *Galimard* (2013), http://www.gallimard.fr/Catalogue/GALLIMARD/Folio/Folio/Eloge-des-frontieres.

From the euro's very launch in 2000, Debray anticipated the single currency's present troubles. In "We Are Our Currency," he lampooned Brussels technocrats as fumbled to select a common image to put on euro bills and coins that would convey a cultural unity that wasn't there. He noted that the classical architectural features of windows and bridges chosen to illustrate openness and connection on the currency were purposefully devoid of any national context or recognizable figures—such as Mao on Chinese currency or George Washington, Thomas Jefferson, and Abraham Lincoln on US currency—who could mark the binding memories that make up the "imaginary space" of nations. By avoiding reference to any national identity, the new European space they portrayed, as Debray put it, was a "no man's land." The euro today may be the most outstanding metaphor of the anti-globalization backlash: commerce can't undo culture, but culture can undo commerce. See Regis Debray, "We Are Our Currency: The Euro and Europe," *New Perspectives Quarterly* 16, no. 1 (Winter 1999): 42–44.

CHAPTER 2

1. Fernando Henrique Cardoso, "Brazil's Crisis Reflects Demise of Representative Democracy across the West," *Huffington Post,*

September 5, 2016, http://www.huffingtonpost.com/fernando-henrique-cardoso/brazils-crisis-reflects-demise-of-democracy_b_11867368.html?utm_hp_ref=world.

2. Moises Naim, *The End of Power* (New York: Basic Books, 2013), 1–2.

3. Naim, *End of Power*, 243–44.

4. Francis Fukuyama, *Political Order and Political Decay: From the Industrial Revolution to the Globalization of Democracy* (New York: Farrar, Strauss & Giroux, 2014), 490–91.

5. Julian Baggini, "Europe's Worst Crisis in Decades Is Also Populism's Greatest Opportunity," *The WorldPost*, July 20, 2015, http://www.huffingtonpost.com/julian-baggini/europe-crisis-populism_b_7812252.html.

6. Amanda Taub and Max Fisher, "Why Referendums Aren't As Democratic As They Seem," *New York Times*, October 4, 2016, https://www.nytimes.com/2016/10/05/world/americas/colombia-brexit-referendum-farc-cameron-santos.html?hp&action=click&pgtype=Homepage&clickSource=story-heading&module=second-column-region&region=top-news&WT.nav=top-news.

7. Kenneth Rogoff, "Britain's Democratic Failure," Project Syndicate, June 2016, https://www.project-syndicate.org/commentary/brexit-democratic-failure-for-uk-by-kenneth-rogoff-2016–06.

8. Berggruen and Gardels, *Intelligent Governance for the 21st Century*, 76.

9. Wael Ghonim, quoted in Thomas L. Friedman, "Social Media: Destroyer or Creator?" *New York Times*, February 3, 2016, http://www.nytimes.com/2016/02/03/opinion/social-media-destroyer-or-creator.html?_r=0.

10. Yasmin Nouh, "Wael Ghonim's Quest to 'Liberate the Internet,'" *The WorldPost*, February 26, 2016, http://www.huffingtonpost.com/entry/wael-ghonim-parlio_us_56d0661e4b03260bf766a32.

11. Nouh, "Wael Ghonim's Quest."

12. Philip Petit, "Depoliticizing Democracy," *Ratio Juris* 17, no. 1 (March 2004): 52–65.

13. Onora O'Neill, "The Age of the Cyber Romantics Is Coming to an End," *The WorldPost*, October 4, 2017, https://www.washingtonpost

.com/news/theworldpost/wp/2017/10/04/the-age-of-the-cyber-romantics-is-coming-to-an-end/?utm_term=.6159b9fc340b.

14. Kate Connolly, "Angela Merkel: Internet Search Engines Are 'Distorting Perception,'" *The Guardian,* October 27, 2016, https://www .theguardian.com/world/2016/oct/27/angela-merkel-internet-search-engines-are-distorting-our-perception.

15. Bernhard Rohleder, "Germany Set Out to Delete Hate Speech Online; Instead, It Made Things Worse," *The WorldPost,* February 20, 2018, https://www.washingtonpost.com/news/theworldpost/wp/2018 /02/20/netzdg/?utm_term=.6aeae1b69a6e.

16. Andrew Rettman and Aleksandra Eriksson, "Germany Calls for EU Laws on Hate Speech and Fake News," *EUobserver,* April 6, 2017, https://euobserver.com/foreign/137521

17. Andrew Keen, "A Safety Belt for the Internet," *The WorldPost,* April 23, 2018, https://www.washingtonpost.com/news/theworldpost /wp/2018/04/23/silicon-valley/?utm_term=.89115dc2118f.

18. Dylan Svoboda, "Hot on the Trail of the 'Bots,'" *Capital Weekly,* May 11, 2018, http://capitolweekly.net/hot-trail-bots/.

19. Kara Swisher and Kurt Wagner, "Facebook's Mark Zuckerberg Wrote a 6,000-Word Letter Addressing Fake News and Saving the World," *Recode.net,* February 16, 2017, https://www.recode.net/2017/2/16 /14632726/mark-zuckerberg-facebook-manifesto-fake-news-terrorism.

20. Eric Schmidt, comments at "Governing the Digital Society" roundtable in Montreal, Quebec, Canada, September 15, 2016.

21. Memo: "Renovating Democracy" working group, 21st Century Council, Lisbon, Portugal, April 16, 2017.

22. Avid Ovadya, "What's Worse Than Fake News? The Distortion of Reality Itself," *The WorldPost,* February 22, 2018, https://www .washingtonpost.com/news/theworldpost/wp/2018/02/22/digital-reality /?utm_term=.c64440f53eb9.

23. Daniel Dennett, "Fake News Isn't the Greatest Threat to Democracy; Total Transparency Is," *The WorldPost,* March 31, 2017, http://www.huffingtonpost.com/entry/fake-news-transparency-trump_us_58dd8a54e4b0e6ac7093b460?cbmfae49z0gs24kj4i&section =us_world.

24. James Madison, "The Federalist Papers: No 10" (1787), The Avalon Project, Lillian Goldman Law Library, Yale Law School, http://avalon.law.yale.edu/18th_century/fed10.asp.

25. Didi Kuo, "Polarization and Partisanship," *The American Interest* 11, no. 2 (October 10, 2015), https://www.the-american-interest.com /2015/10/10/polarization-and-partisanship/.

26. John Gramlich, "How Countries around the World View Democracy, Military Rule, and Other Political Systems," Pew Research Center, October 30, 2017, http://www.pewresearch.org/fact-tank/2017 /10/30/global-views-political-systems/.

27. Duncan Robinson, "Rise of Pop-Up Parties Throws Netherlands Poll Wide Open," *Financial Times,* February 17, 2017.

28. Davide Casaleggio, "A Top Leader of Italy's Five Star Movement: Why We Won," *The WorldPost,* March 19, 2018, https://www .washingtonpost.com/news/theworldpost/wp/2018/03/19/ five-star/?utm_term=.839b3588d793

29. Casaleggio, "A Top Leader of Italy's Five Star Movement." See Rousseau's website, https://rousseau.movimento5stelle.it.

30. See "Tackling Populism: Hope over Fear," 1989 Generation Initiative, 2017, http://1989generationinitiative.org/wp-content/uploads /2017/11/Final-Policy-Booklet_2017.pdf

31. Carl J. Richard, *The Founders and the Classics: Greece, Rome, and the American Enlightenment* (Cambridge: Cambridge University Press, 1994), 111.

32. Madison, "Federalist Papers: No 10."

33. John Adams to John Taylor, December 17, 1814, Founders Online, National Archives, https://founders.archives.gov/documents/Adams /99-02-02-6371.

34. Thomas Jefferson to John Adams, October 28, 1813, in *The Founders' Constitution,* ed. Philip B. Kurland and Ralph Lerner (Chicago: University of Chicago Press; Carmel, IN: Liberty Fund), http://press-pubs.uchicago.edu/founders/documents/v1ch15s61.html.

35. James Madison, "Federalist Papers: No. 47," The Avalon Project, Lillian Goldman Law Library, Yale Law School, http://avalon.law.yale .edu/18th_century/fed47.asp.

36. John Adams, *Loose Thoughts on Government* (1776), in *American Archives*, ed. Peter Force, 4th series (Washington, DC: M. St. Clair Clarke and Peter Force, 1837–53), vol. 6, p. 711; Adams, *Thoughts on Government*, in *Works of John Adams, Second President of the United States*, ed. Charles Francis Adams (Boston: C.C. Little and J. Brown, 1850–56), vol. 4, pp. 196, 195.

37. Adams, *Thoughts on Government*, 4: 196, 195.

38. Hamilton, Pay Book of the State Company of Artillery, 1777, in *The Papers of Alexander Hamilton*, ed. Harold C. Syrett and Jacob E. Cooke (New York: Columbia University Press, 1961), vol. 1, p. 397.

39. James Madison, "Federalist Papers: No. 63" (1788), The Avalon Project, Lillian Goldman Law Library, Yale Law School, http://avalon.law.yale.edu/18th_century/fed63.asp.

40. John C. Calhoun, *A Disquisition on Government* (Columbia, SC: A.S. Johnson, 1851), 58ff, available at Internet Archive, https://archive.org/details/adisquisitionono0ocalgoog.

41. C.H. Hoebeke, *The Road to Mass Democracy* (New Brunswick, NJ: Transaction, 1995), 47.

42. Calhoun, *A Disquisition on Government*, 58ff.

43. Madison, "Federalist Papers: No. 10."

44. Ganesh Sitaraman, *The Crisis of the Middle Class Constitution: Why Economic Inequality Threatens Our Republic* (New York: Alfred A. Knopf, 2017), 29.

45. Mark Twain and Charles Dudley Warner, *The Gilded Age: A Tale of Today* (Hartford, CT: American Publishing Company, 1873).

46. Hazen S. Pingree, "A Letter to Professor George Gunton," in Chicago Conference on Trusts, *Chicago Conference on Trusts: Speeches, Debates, Resolutions, Lists of the Delegates, Committees, Etc., Held September 13th, 14th, 15th, 16th, 1899* (Chicago: Civic Federation of Chicago, 1900), 598.

47. As historian Hasia Diner has written: "Some populists believed that Jews made up a class of international financiers whose policies had ruined small family farms, they asserted, owned the banks and promoted the gold standard, the chief sources of their impoverishment. Agrarian populism posited the city as antithetical to American values,

asserting that Jews were the essence of urban corruption." Hasia R. Diner, *The Jews of the United States, 1654 to 2000* (Berkeley: University of California Press, 2004), 170.

48. Although Wisconsin now has the referendum, it never actually enacted the ballot initiative, which La Follette had proposed, because of a particular circumstance of legislative fatigue in 1914 after passing a large tax increase for public works and other measures on its long list of reforms.

49. Roosevelt, introduction to Charles McCarthy, *The Wisconsin Idea* (New York: Macmillan, 1912), vii.

50. "The Wisconsin Idea," University of Wisconsin–Madison, http://www.wisc.edu/wisconsin-idea/.

51. Stevenson quoted in Jack Stark, "The Wisconsin Idea: The University's Service to the State," in Wisconsin Blue Book (Madison: Wisconsin Legislative Reference Bureau, 1995–96), PDF, 1–80.

52. Walter Lippmann, *Public Opinion* (1921; reprinted, Brooklyn, NY: Feather Press, 2010), 224.

53. Temperance was another key facet of the Progressive movement: the Eighteenth Amendment instituted Prohibition.

54. Alexis de Tocqueville, *Democracy in America*, chapter 13, American Studies, University of Virginia, http://xroads.virginia.edu/~hyper /detoc/1_ch13.htm.

55. Voters in Switzerland, the country from which the initiative had been adopted, did not approve women's right to vote until 1971. Daniel A. Smith and Caroline J. Tolbert, *Educated by Initiative: The Effect of Direct Democracy on Citizens and Political Organizations* (Ann Arbor: University of Michigan Press, 2004), 28.

56. Smith and Tolbert, *Educated by Initiative*, 29.

57. "California Proposition 23, the Suspension of AB 32," *Ballotpedia*, https://ballotpedia.org/California_Proposition_23,_the_Suspension_ of_AB_32_(2010).

58. These numbers will vary from election to election as they depend on the turnout in previous elections.

59. While many assume such consultants arose only recently in the game of direct democracy, they actually appeared very early on.

The first professional campaign-management firm in the United States, Campaign Inc., also known as Whittaker & Baxter, was established in the 1930s to specialize in California ballot initiatives.

60. Eric Lipton and Robert Faturechi, "The Officials Write Ballot Questions; Companies Write Them Checks," *New York Time,* May 11, 2016, http://www.nytimes.com/2016/11/05/us/politics/secretaries-of-state-elections-ballot-initiatives.html?_r=0%20Proposals%20in%20 California%20and%20elsewhere.

61. One response that the Think Long Committee in California has considered is assigning the writing of the ballot summary to a nonpartisan committee.

62. Phillip L. Dubois and Floyd Feeney, *Lawmaking by Initiative: Issues, Options and Comparisons* (Bronx, NY: Agathon Press, 1998), available on Google Books, https://books.google.ch/books?id=Rq18JkGtj6IC &printsec=copyright&hl=de&source=gbs_pub_info_r#v=onepage& q&f=false.

63. Another prime example of the unintended consequences of governing by ballot initiative was the "Three Strikes Law," passed by 72 per cent of California voters in 1994. It mandated that any "persistent offender" who committed three felonies would receive a sentence of life imprisonment. The prison population predictably swelled from 125,000 in 1994 to 165,000 by 2010. Already by 1999, the number of drug offenders imprisoned in the state was more than twice the number of inmates who were imprisoned for all crimes in 1978. California's became the biggest prison system in the Western industrialized world, a system 40 percent bigger than the Federal Bureau of Prisons. The state held more inmates in its jails and prisons than did France, Great Britain, Germany, Japan, Singapore, and the Netherlands combined. (Eric Schlosser, "The Prison Industrial Complex," *The Atlantic* (December 1998), http://www.theatlantic.com/magazine/archive/1998 /12/the-prison-industrial-complex/304669/). Because of the costs associated with this inmate explosion—exacerbated by the political clout of the prison guard unions to secure generous benefits— California was soon spending more on prisons than on public higher education. In 2011, prisons and higher education accounted for

11 percent and 7.5 percent of the state budget, respectively (Berggruen and Gardels, *Intelligent Governance for the 21st Century*) At the time of this writing, California spends almost $71,000 per year for each incarcerated inmate. (Matt Krupnick, "Californians Pay for State's Public Colleges but Increasingly Can't Get In," *PBS News Hour,* August 20, 2015, http://www.pbs.org/newshour/updates/californians-pay-states-public-colleges-increasingly-cant-get/.) Because no new taxes were raised to build more prisons, the existing ones became grossly over-crowded, to the point that in 2011 the US Supreme Court charged California with violating prisoners' human rights and ordered the release of 30,000 inmates. (Adam Liptak, "Justices 5–4, Tell California to Cut Prisoner Population," *New York Times,* May 24, 2011, http://www.nytimes.com/2011/05/24/us/24scotus.html.) As these long-term consequences of the 1994 Three Strikes Law were finally acknowledged nearly twenty years on, two new ballot initiatives in 2014 and 2016 eased the costs and crowding by "realigning" the states' criminal justice responsibilities. The initiatives devolved many of those responsibilities on the counties (also shifting the fiscal strain on to them) and narrowed the mandatory sentencing criteria to cases of violent crime.

64. Mark Baldassare, "At Issue: Improving California's Democracy," Public Policy Institute, 2012, http://www.ppic.org/content/pubs/atissue/AI_1012MBAI.pdf.

65. Berggruen and Gardels, *Intelligent Governance for the 21st Century,* 133.

66. "The Ungovernable State," *The Economist,* February 19, 2009, http://www.economist.com/node/13145207 ("ungovernable"); "The Perils of Extreme Democracy," *The Economist,* April 20, 2011, http://www.economist.com/node/18586520.

67. A simple-majority vote by the legislature can place statutory measures on the ballot; a two-thirds vote is required for constitutional amendments.

68. Members included two legendary former Speakers of the state assembly, Robert Hertzberg and Willie Brown; former chief justice of the California Supreme Court Ronald George; President Bill Clinton's top economic adviser, Laura Tyson; Alphabet/Google chief Eric

Schmidt; former state treasurer Matthew Fong; Latina community advocate Antonia Hernandez; labor leader Maria Elena Durazo; former governor Gray Davis; former Warner Brothers and Yahoo chief Terry Semel; philanthropist Eli Broad; and the two former US secretaries of state who hail from California, George Shultz and Condoleezza Rice. The group was staffed by former Republican and Democratic state finance directors. At the very first meeting, then-governor Schwarzenegger sat at the head of the table with the former governor he had ousted, Gray Davis. The message was clear: California's problems were not the fault of any political leader alone, but of a broken system. Later, incoming governor Jerry Brown would testify before the committee, as would the state treasurer, the legislative analyst, the leaders of the legislature, the mayors of San Francisco and Los Angeles, the heads of the teachers' union, and an array of economists and policy experts.

69. Berggruen and Gardels, *Intelligent Governance for the 21st Century,* 130.

70. The proposal echoes an idea floated some years ago by the late Harvard sociologist Daniel Bell, who called for a "third house" in the US Congress. He argued that term limits should be imposed on all members of the US House and Senate and that "experienced and disinterested" former senators and representatives would then join a third house, the "House of Counselors." There they would provide a pool of expertise for "commissions and independent bodies" to evaluate policies from a common good instead of a constituency perspective. Daniel A. Bell, *East Meets West: Human Rights and Democracy in East Asia* (Princeton: Princeton University Press, 2000), 324.

71. "How Italy's 5 Star Movement Enables Democratic Participation Online," *The WorldPost* YouTube Channel, August 1, 2017, https://www.youtube.com/watch?v=Ejc-ssaz84A.

72. Davide Casaleggio, "How Italians Learned to Govern Themselves through Technology," *The WorldPost,* March 22, 2017, http://www.huffingtonpost.com/entry/five-star-movement-internet_us_58c b008ae4b0be71dcf3048d?px5zk8c6k31w3tyb9&section=us_world.

73. House of Lords, Select Committee on Artificial Intelligence, Report of Session 2017–19, https://publications.parliament.uk/pa

/ld201719/ldselect/ldai/100/100.pdf. Despite its reputation as a bastion of privilege, which it was for centuries, the House of Lords is actually now more diverse than the House of Commons, the *Guardian* reports, with more women, blacks, ethnic minorities and disabled than the elected body. See Colin Low, "Lords Reform: The Lords Is More Diverse and Democratic than the Commons," *The Guardian,* July 9, 2012,https://www.theguardian.com/commentisfree/2012/jul/09/house-of-lords-commons-democracy.

74. Berggruen and Gardels, *Intelligent Governance for the 21st Century,* 135.

CHAPTER 3

Epigraph: Alexander Kaufman, "Stephen Hawking Says We Should Really Be Scared of Capitalism, Not Robots," *The WorldPost,* October 8, 2015, http://www.huffingtonpost.com/entry/stephen-hawking-capitalism-robots_us_5616c20ce4b0dbb8000d9f15.

1. Chris Weller, "Elon Musk Doubles Down on Universal Basic Income: 'It's Going to Be Necessary,'" *Business Insider,* February 13, 2017, http://www.businessinsider.com/elon-musk-universal-basic-income-2017-2.

2. Laura Tyson and Michael Spence, "Exploring the Effects of Technology on Income and Wealth Inequality," in *After Piketty: The Agenda for Economics and Inequality,* ed. Heather Boushey, J. Bradford DeLong, and Marshall Steinbaum (Cambridge, MA: Harvard University Press, 2017), ch. 8.

3. Erik Brynjolfsson and Andrew McAfee, "Jobs, Productivity, and the Great Decoupling," *New York Times,* December 12, 2012, http://www.nytimes.com/2012/12/12/opinion/global/jobs-productivity-and-the-great-decoupling.html.

4. Daniel Griswold, "Globalization Isn't Killing Factory Jobs; Trade Is Actually Why Manufacturing Is Up 40%," *Los Angeles Times,* August 1, 2016, http://www.latimes.com/opinion/op-ed/la-oe-griswold-globalization-and-trade-help-manufacturing-20160801-snap-story.html.

5. Benedikt Frey and Michael A. Osborne, "The Future of Employment: How Susceptible Are Jobs to Computerisation?" September 17, 2013, http://www.oxfordmartin.ox.ac.uk/downloads/academic/The_Future_of_Employment.pdf.

6. Frey and Osborne, "The Future of Employment."

7. Gavin Jackson, "Job Loss Fears from Automation Overblown, Says OECD," *Financial Times,* April 1, 2018, https://www.ft.com/content/732c3b78–329f-11e8-b5bf-23cb17fd1498.

8. Tyson and Spence, "Exploring the Effects of Technology on Income and Wealth Inequality."

9. Larry Summers, "The Case for Expansion," *Financial Times* (October 8, 2015), 9.

10. Kenneth P. Thomas, *Capital beyond Borders: States and Firms in the Auto Industry, 1960–94* (New York: Macmillan, 1997), 89.

11. Company Info, Facebook Newsroom, https://newsroom.fb.com/company-info/; "Number of Facebook Employees from 2004 to 2017 (Full-Time), *Statista,* https://www.statista.com/statistics/273563/number-of-facebook-employees/.

12. Paul Mason, *Postcapitalism: A Guide to Our Future* (New York: Farrar, Strauss and Giroux, 2015), 139.

13. James Manyika et al., "Unlocking the Potential of the Internet of Things," McKinsey Global Institute, June 2015, http://www.mckinsey.com/business-functions/business-technology/our-insights/the-internet-of-things-the-value-of-digitizing-the-physical-world.

14. Gerald Raunig, "A Few Fragments on Machines," EIPCP (European Institute for Progressive Cultural Policies), October 2005, http://eipcp.net/transversal/1106/raunig/en/#_ftn3.

15. Benjamin Kunkel, "Marx's Revenge," *The Nation,* February 8, 2017, https://www.thenation.com/article/marxs-revenge/.

16. David Runciman, "A Worthy Successor to Marx?" review of *Postcapitalism: A Guide to Your Future,* by Paul Mason, *The Guardian,* August 15, 2015, https://www.theguardian.com/books/2015/aug/15/post-capitalism-by-paul-mason-review-worthy-successor-to-marx.

17. Slavoj Žižek, *First as Tragedy, Then as Farce* (London: Verso, 2009), 145–47.

18. Erik Brynjolfsson, interview by Nathan Gardels, August 25, 2016.

19. Tyson and Spence, "Exploring the Effects of Technology on Income and Wealth Inequality."

20. Nathan Gardels, "You Can Manufacture What You Desire," *The WorldPost,* March 2, 2015, http://www.huffingtonpost.com/2015/03/02 /manufacture-your-desire_n_6777606.html.

21. Lisa Eadicicco, "These Are the Most Popular iPhone Apps of 2016," *Time* Magazine, December 6, 2016, http://time.com/4592864 /most-popular-iphone-apps-2016/.

22. Is dematerialization real? Vaclav Smil, the contrarian polymath whom Bill Gates has called his "guru," studies the interdependence of technology, the human population, and the environment. He regards dematerialization with a dash of skepticism. Technology has certainly enabled a "relative dematerialization," he says—the use of lighter, less expensive materials and more efficient use of resources in particular circumstances. But these impressive achievements do not translate into *absolute* declines in resource use on a global scale. In fact, just the opposite: because technological advances have made goods cheaper, mass-producible, and more readily available for widespread use, and because human nature always yearns for "better," material consumption has vastly *increased.* Although new technologies may be efficient in and of themselves, they end up generating *more* demand, not less. In the end, the knowledge economy remains based on microprocessors that are composed of mined materials that must be forged with energy inputs, and that use electricity to operate (that is, until synthetic biology can create organic processors and until renewable energy replaces scarce fossil fuel generation). See Nathan Gardels, "Bill Gates' Guru: 'I'm Not Impressed with Silicon Valley'; 'I Don't Have a Cell Phone'; 'I Never Blog.' *The WorldPost,* July 14, 2017, http://www.huffingtonpost .com/nathan-gardels/vaclav-smil-interview_b_5584909.html.

23. Michael Spence, *The Next Convergence: The Future of Economic Growth in a Multispeed World* (New York: Picador, 2012).

24. Tyson and Spence, "Exploring the Effects of Technology on Income and Wealth Inequality."

25. Jeremy Rifkin, *The Third Industrial Revolution* (London: Palgrave Macmillan, 2011).

26. Alvin Toffler and Heidi Toffler, *Revolutionary Wealth: How It Will Be Created and How It Will Change Our Lives* (New York: Alfred A. Knopf, 2007).

27. Vanessa Bates Ramirez, "How Robots Helped Create 100,000 Jobs at Amazon," *Singularity Hub*, February 10, 2017, https://singularityhub .com/2017/02/10/how-robots-helped-create-100000-jobs-at-amazon/.

28. John Chambers, "How Digitizing Europe Will Create 850,000 New Jobs," *The WorldPost*, March 16, 2015, http://www.huffingtonpost .com/john-chambers/digitizing-europe-jobs_b_6873984.html.

29. Mo Ibrahim, phone interview with Nathan Gardels, August 2015.

30. Ed Cropley, "Mobile Phone Access in Africa Set to Double in Next Five Years," Thomson Reuters, June 03, 2015, archived at Next Billion (William Davidson Institute, University of Michigan), http:// nextbillion.net/newspost.aspx?newsid=9987; David Smith, "Internet Use on Mobile Phones in Africa Predicted to Increase 20-Fold," *The Guardian*, June 5, 2014, https://www.theguardian.com/world/2014 /jun/05/internet-use-mobile-phones-africa-predicted-increase-20- fold ("mobile continent").

31. Toby Shapshak, "Africa Tops 500m Mobile Users, Adds $150bn to Continent's Economy," *Forbes*, July 26, 2016, https://www.forbes .com/sites/tobyshapshak/2016/07/26/africa-tops-500m-mobile-users- adds-150bn-to-continents-economy/#16e28f14860e.

32. Gillian Tett, "One Small Step for Gig Economy Workers," *Financial Times*, June 23, 2016, https://next.ft.com/content/09882a8c- 3928–11e6–9a05–82a9b15a8ee7.

33. Robert Reich, "The Sharing Economy Is Hurtling Us Backwards," *Salon.com*, February 4, 2015, http://www.salon.com/2015/02 /04/robert_reich_the_sharing_economy_is_hurtling_us_backwards_ partner/.

34. "Youth Unemployment Rate in EU Member States as of March 2018 (Seasonally Adjusted)," Statista, https://www.statista.com/statistics /266228/youth-unemployment-rate-in-eu-countries/.

35. Quentin Peel, "Merkel Warns of Cost of Welfare," *Financial Times,*December16,2012,http://www.ft.com/intl/cms/s/0/8ccof584–45fa-11e2-b7ba-00144feabdco.html#axzz4BNMCqT27.

36. Mehreen Khan, "German Trade Surplus Swells to Fresh Record," *Financial Times,* May 10, 2016, http://www.ft.com/fastft/2016/05/10/german-current-account-surplus-swells-to-record/.

37. Guy Chazan, "Martin Schulz Takes Aim at 'Sacred Cow' German Economic Reforms," *Financial Times,* February 22, 2017, https://www.ft.com/content/fbfe0290-f823–11e6–9516–2d969e0d3b65.

38. "Minimum Wages," Destatis: Statistiches Bundesamt, 2017, https://www.destatis.de/EN/FactsFigures/NationalEconomyEnvironment/EarningsLabourCosts/MinimumWages/MinimumWages.html.

39. Jeevan Vasagar, "German 'Minijobs' Reforms Fuel Debate on the Price of Inequality," *Financial Times* (August 7, 2015), 4.

40. Anne-Sylvaine Chassany, "Uber: A Route out of the French Banlieues," *Financial Times,* March 3, 2016, http://www.ft.com/intl/cms/s/0/bf3d0444-e129–11e5–9217–6ae3733a2cd1.html#axzz4BNMCqT27.

41. Toomas Ilves, former president of Estonia, interview with Nicolas Berggruen.

42. John Thornhill, "Digital Disruption and the Next 'Innocent Fraud,'" *Financial Times,* October 24, 2016, https://www.ft.com/content/3bbf61d2–99cc-11e6-b8c6–568a43813464.

43. Robert C. Allen, "Engel's Pause: Technical Change, Capital Accumulation, and Inequality in the British Industrial Revolution," *Explorations in Economic History* 46, no. 4 (October 2009), https://doi.org/10.1016/j.eeh.2009.04.004.

44. Thomas Piketty, *Capital in the Twenty-First Century,* trans. Arthur Goldhammer (Cambridge, MA: Harvard University Press, 2013).

45. Anthony B. Atkinson, *Inequality: What Can Be Done?* (Cambridge, MA: Harvard University Press, 2015), 155.

46. Branko Milanovic, "Can Inequality Be Reduced?" *The Globalist,* December 24, 2016, http://www.theglobalist.com/inequality-be-reduced-education-access-income/.

47. Nathan Gardels, "Capitalism's Central Contradiction: The Past Devours the Future," *The WorldPost,* March 24, 2014, http://www

.huffingtonpost.com/nathan-gardels/capitalisms-central-contradiction_
b_5001581.html.

48. "Cal State LA Marked Number One in the Nation for Upward
Mobility," Office of Communications and Public Affairs, California
State University Los Angeles, http://www.calstatela.edu/univ/ppa
/publicat/cal-state-la-ranked-number-one-nation-upward-mobility.

49. Edward D. Kleinbard, "Don't Soak the Rich," *New York Times,*
October 10, 2014, https://www.nytimes.com/2014/10/10/opinion/dont-
soak-the-rich.html?_r=0.

50. "Understanding the Basics," OnePath, http://www.onepath
.com.au/personal-business/superannuation/understanding-the-basics
.aspx.

51. James Rufus Koren, "California Proposal for State-Run Retirement Plan for Private-Sector Workers Moves Forward," *Los Angeles Times,*
March 29, 2016, http://www.latimes.com/business/la-fi-mandatory-401k-
20160329-story.html.

52. "CPF Overview," Central Provident Fund Board, https://www
.cpf.gov.sg/Members/AboutUs/about-us-info/cpf-overview.

53. Atkinson, *Inequality.*

54. Dani Rodrik, "From Welfare State to Innovation State," *Project Syndicate,* January 14, 2015, https://www.project-syndicate.org/commentary
/labor-saving-technology-by-dani-rodrik-2015-01.

55. "Characteristics of Mutual Fund Owners," *2017 Investment Company Fact Book* (Investment Company Institute, 2017), ch. 6, https://
www.ici.org/pdf/2017_factbook.pdf.

56. Sarah O'Brien, "Fed Survey Shows 40 Percent of Americans
Can't Cover a $400 Emergency Expense," CNBC, May 22, 2018,
https://www.cnbc.com/2018/05/22/fed-survey-40-percent-of-adults-
cant-cover-400-emergency-expense.html.

57. Sarah Kessler, "Lawrence Summers Says Bill Gates' Idea of a
Robot Tax Is 'Profoundly Misguided,'" *Quartz,* March 2017, https://
qz.com/925412/lawrence-summers-says-bill-gates-idea-for-a-robot-tax-
is-profoundly-misguided/.

58. Eric Schmidt, conversation with Berggruen Institute 21st Century Council, meeting at Carlyle Hotel, New York, December 1, 2016.

59. "Government Pension Fund Global: The Fund," Norges Bank Investment Management, https://www.nbim.no/en/the-fund/.

60. Chris Weller, "Elon Musk Doubles Down on Universal Basic Income: 'It's Going to Be Necessary,'" *Business Insider*, February 13, 2017, http://www.businessinsider.com/elon-musk-universal-basic-income-2017-2.

61. "Basically Unaffordable," *The Economist*, May 23, 2015, http://www.economist.com/news/finance-and-economics/21651897-replacing-welfare-payments-basic-income-all-alluring.

62. Patricia Laya, "Mexico's Richest Man Wants a Three-Day Workweek," *Bloomberg BusinessWeek*, August 4, 2016, https://www.bloomberg.com/news/articles/2016-08-04/mexico-s-richest-man-wants-a-three-day-workweek.

63. John Maynard Keynes, "Economic Possibilities for our Grandchildren," in *Essays in Persuasion* (New York: W. W. Norton, 1963), 358–73.

64. Michael Shields, "Lower Saxony Buys VW Shares to Keep 20 Pct Stake," *Reuters*, May 29, 2007, http://www.reuters.com/article/2007/05/29/idUSL2961827120070529.

CHAPTER 4

Epigraph: Graham Allison and Robert Blackwill, "Interview: Lee Kuan Yew on the Future of U.S.-China Relations," *The Atlantic*, March 5, 2013, https://www.theatlantic.com/china/archive/2013/03/interview-lee-kuan-yew-on-the-future-of-us-china-relations/273657/.

1. The first took place in November 2013, the second in November 2015; the third is scheduled for March 2018.

2. Yi Wang, "Meet the Mastermind behind Xi Jinping's Power," *The WorldPost*, https://www.washingtonpost.com/news/theworldpost/wp/2017/11/06/wang-huning/?utm_term=.3f362d2ee3d7.

3. "Capitalism Has No Patent Right over the Market," interview with Hu Qili by Nathan Gardels, *New Perspectives Quarterly*, 5, no. 4 (Winter 1988–89).

4. "Xi Jinping," China.org.cn, http://www.china.org.cn/china/leadership/2013-03/16/content_28193070.htm.

5. Rhitu Chatterjee, "In India, Access to Toilets Remains a Huge Problem—Worst of All for Women and Girls," *The World*, Public Radio International, May 12, 2016, https://www.pri.org/stories/2016–05–12/india-access-toilets-remains-huge-problem-worst-all-women-and-girls.

6. Jamil Anderlini and Wang Feng, "Xi Jinping Delivers Robust Defence of Globalisation at Davos," *Financial Times*, January 17, 2017, https://www.ft.com/content/67ec2ec0-dca2–11e6–9d7c-be108f1c1dce.

7. The Party communique announcing Xi's elevation took care to note that his power still had limits: he remained subject to party supervision and the established codes of collective leadership. "No organization or individual can be permitted for any reason to run counter to this system," it said. It went on to caution that propaganda related to leaders should "derive truth from facts" and, remembering Mao's mistakes, insisted that "adulation is forbidden" (禁止吹捧, *jinzhi chuipeng*).

8. Kai-Fu Lee, "The Real Threat of Artificial Intelligence," *New York Times*, June 24, 2017, https://www.nytimes.com/2017/06/24/opinion/sunday/artificial-intelligence-economic-inequality.html?_r=0.

9. Edward Tse, "Inside China's Quest to Become the Global Leader in AI," *The WorldPost*, October 19, 2017, https://www.washingtonpost.com/news/theworldpost/wp/2017/10/19/inside-chinas-quest-to-become-the-global-leader-in-ai/?utm_term=.355887df76d7.

10. Scott Kennedy, "Made in China 2025," CSIS (Center for Strategic and International Studies), June 1, 2015, https://www.csis.org/analysis/made-china-2025.

11. "Industrie 4.0," GTAI: Germany Trade & Invest, https://www.gtai.de/GTAI/Navigation/EN/Invest/Industries/Industrie-4-0/Industrie-4-0/industrie-4-0-what-is-it.html.

12. "New Business Deals Signed as Merkel Wraps up China Trip," *DW (Deutsche Welle)*, October 30, 2015, http://www.dw.com/en/new-business-deals-signed-as-merkel-wraps-up-china-trip/a-18817481.

13. Nathan Gardels, "How Tech May Trip the Thucydides Trap," *The WorldPost*, May 18, 2018, https://www.washingtonpost.com/news/theworldpost/wp/2018/05/18/china-technology-2/?utm_term=.1745a45dca16.

14. Jamil Anderlini, "China: Overborrowed and Overbuilt," *Financial Times,* January 29, 2015, https://www.ft.com/content/8b2ce9c4-a2ed-11e4-9c06-00144feab7de.

15. "China Hit by First Moody's Downgrade since 1989 on Debt Risk," *Bloomberg News,* May 23, 2017, https://www.bloomberg.com/news/articles/2017-05-24/china-downgraded-to-a1-by-moody-s-on-worsening-debt-outlook.

16. Fred Hu, "Why It Is a Loser's Game to Bet against China's Leadership," *The WorldPost,* August, 26, 2015, http://www.huffingtonpost.com/fred-hu/china-leadership-stock-market_b_8043358.html.

17. Yang Yao, "The Disinterested Government," China Center for Economic Research, Peking University, October 31, 2008, http://policydialogue.org/files/events/Yao_Disinterested_Government_China.pdf.

18. Mancur Olson, *The Rise and Decline of Nations: Economic Growth, Stagflation, and Social Rigidities* (New Haven: Yale University Press, 1982). 74.

19. Richard Wike and Bruce Stokes, "China and the World," Pew Research Center, October 5, 2016, http://www.pewglobal.org/2015/09/24/corruption-pollution-inequality-are-top-concerns-in-china/.

20. Bruce W. Nelan, "What They Said in Private," CNN, November 10, 1997, http://www.cnn.com/ALLPOLITICS/1997/11/03/time/jiang.html.

21. Kevin Rudd, "Summary Report: U.S.-China 21," Belfer Center for Science and International Affairs, Harvard Kennedy School, April 2015, http://www.belfercenter.org/publication/summary-report-us-china-21.

22. Berggruen and Gardels, *Intelligent Governance for the 21st Century,* 55.

23. Andy Kiersz, "This Map Shows Where People Are Most Satisfied with Their Country's Direction, *Business Insider,* February 25, 2014, http://www.businessinsider.com/pew-research-global-satisfaction-map-2014-2.

24. Richard Wike and Bridget Parker, "Corruption, Pollution, Inequality Are Top Concerns in China," Pew Research Center, September

24, 2015, http://www.pewglobal.org/2015/09/24/corruption-pollution-inequality-are-top-concerns-in-china/.

25. Antonio Gramsci, *Further Selections from the Prison Notebooks* (Minneapolis: University of Minnesota Press, 1995).

26. Joseph S. Nye, *Soft Power: The Means to Success in World Politics* (New York: PublicAffairs, 2004).

27. Some China scholars disagree with this view and see it as selective memory that serves the Communist Party's purpose. See Jeffrey Wasserstrom and Kate Merkel-Hess, "Xi Jinping's Authoritarianism Does a Disservice to China's Nuanced Political Tradition," *The World-Post,* September 28, 2016, http://www.huffingtonpost.com/jeffrey-wasserstrom/xi-jinping-authoritarian_b_11778782.html.

28. *Encyclopaedia Britannica* (online), s.v. "Legalism" (revised and updated 2008), https://www.britannica.com/topic/Legalism.

29. Zheng Yongnian, *The Chinese Communist Party as Organizational Emperor: Culture, Reproduction and Transformation* (Abingdon, UK: Routledge, 2010).

30. John Keane, "Phantom Democracy: A Puzzle at the Heart of Chinese Politics," *South China Morning Post,* August 25, 2018, https://www.scmp.com/week-asia/politics/article/2161276/phantom-democracy-puzzle-heart-chinese-politics.

31. The Party under Xi can be startlingly unconventional and pragmatic. For example, while there is no traditional basis in China for an independent judiciary, recent reforms have set up independent county-level courts designed to be free from the influence of corrupt local Party bosses.

32. Steven Mufson, "This Documentary Went Viral in China, Then It Was Censored; It Won't be Forgotten," *Washington Post,* March 16, 2015, https://www.washingtonpost.com/news/energy-environment/wp/2015/03/16/this-documentary-went-viral-in-china-then-it-was-censored-it-wont-be-forgotten/?utm_term=.ee8835504885.

33. Paul Carsten, "China Will Spend $182 Billion to Boost Internet Speed by the End of 2017," *Business Insider,* May 20, 2015, http://www.businessinsider.com/r-china-to-spend-182-billion-to-boost-internet-by-end-of-2017-2015-5.

34. Yuan Yang, "Multinationals in China Brace for Online Crackdown," *Financial Times*, July 31, 2017, https://www.ft.com/content/cb4bec0a-75b6-11e7-90c0-90a9d1bc9691.

35. Josh Chin and Gillian Wong, "China's New Tool for Social Control: A Credit Rating for Everything," *Wall Street Journal*, November 28, 2016, http://www.wsj.com/articles/chinas-new-tool-for-social-control-a-credit-rating-for-everything-1480351590

36. George Yeo, "Why Singapore at 50 Is like a Banyan Tree, a Bonsai, and Nanotechnology," *The WorldPost*, August 3, 2015, http://www.huffingtonpost.com/george-yeo/singapore-at-50_b_7921632.html?utm_hp_ref=world.

37. Kishore Mahbubani, "Figuring Out the Right Path for Political Evolution," *Straits Times*, July 22, 2017, http://www.straitstimes.com/opinion/figuring-out-the-right-path-for-political-evolution.

38. Tom Phillips, "China Rejects Tribunal's Ruling in South China Sea Case," *The Guardian*, July 12, 2016, https://www.theguardian.com/world/2016/jul/12/philippines-wins-south-china-sea-case-against-china.

39. Richard Javad Heydarian, "Here's Why the South China Sea Dispute Will Continue to Haunt Philippine-China Relations," *The WorldPost*, July 25, 2017, http://www.huffingtonpost.com/entry/south-china-sea-dispute-duterte_us_597603aae4b09e5f6cd0d53b.

40. Zheng Bijian, "China's 'One Belt, One Road' Plan Marks the Next Phase of Globalization," *The WorldPost*, May 18, 2017, http://www.huffingtonpost.com/entry/china-one-belt-one-road_us_591c6b41e4boed14cddb4527.

41. Zhao Tingyang, "Can This Ancient Chinese Philosophy Save Us from Global Chaos?" *The WorldPost*, February 7, 2018, https://www.washingtonpost.com/news/theworldpost/wp/2018/02/07/tianxia/?utm_term=.3aacbd3599c4.

42. Zhao, "Can This Ancient Chinese Philosophy Save Us from Global Chaos?"

43. Nathan Gardels, "The Return of the Middle Kingdom in a Post-American World," *New Perspectives Quarterly* 25, no. 4 (Fall 2009), https://doi.org/10.1111/j.1540-5842.2008.01015.x.

44. Stephen S. Roach, "Rethinking the Next China," Project Syndicate, May 25, 2017, https://www.project-syndicate.org/commentary/global-china-risks-and-opportunities-by-stephen-s--roach-2017–05.

45. George Yeo, "China's Grand Design: Pivot to Eurasia," *The Globalist*, November 8, 2015, http://www.theglobalist.com/china-economy-gdp-asia/.

46. Nathan Gardels, "China's New Silk Road May Be a Game Changer for Pakistan," *The WorldPost*, August 17, 2016, http://www.huffingtonpost.com/entry/china-silk-road-pakistan-shaukat-aziz_us_57b49a98e4b0b42c38afc54a.

47. Peter Doimi de Frankopan, "These Days, All Roads Lead to Beijing," *The WorldPost*, July 28, 2017, http://www.huffingtonpost.com/entry/china-silk-road_us_5978d667e4b0a8a40e84cec7.

48. Raghuram Rajan, interview with Nathan Gardels, October 2017 in Agenda and Report for Annual Meeting of the 21st Century Council, Briefing Book, December 2017.

49. Brahma Challaney, "China's Creditor Imperialism," Project Syndicate, December 20, 2017, https://www.project-syndicate.org/commentary/china-sri-lanka-hambantota-port-debt-by-brahma-chellaney-2017–12?barrier=accesspaylog.

50. "Mahathir Mohamad Warns against 'New Colonialism' during China Visit," *Financial Times*, August 20, 2018, https://www.ft.com/content/7566599e-a443–11e8–8ecf-a7ae1beff35b.

51. Nathan Gardels, "Trump's 'America First' Meets China's 'Community of Common Destiny,'" February 9, 2018, https://www.washingtonpost.com/news/theworldpost/wp/2018/02/09/america-first/?utm_term=.9e672c333eec.

52. Dani Rodrik, "The Inescapable Trilemma of the World Economy," Dani Rodrik's Weblog, June 27, 2007, http://rodrik.typepad.com/dani_rodriks_weblog/2007/06/the-inescapable.html.

53. Nathan Gardels, "The U.S.-China Trade War May Kill the WTO; and That Is a Good Thing," *The WorldPost*, August 24, 2018, https://www.washingtonpost.com/news/theworldpost/wp/2018/08/24/china-trade/?utm_term=.0dab01a71188.

54. Dani Rodrik, "Put Globalization to Work for Democracies," *New York Times*, September 9, 2016, https://www.nytimes.com/2016/09

/18/opinion/sunday/put-globalization-to-work-for-democracies.html?
smprod=nytcore-iphone&smid=nytcore-iphone-share&_r=1.

55. Ernesto Zedillo, quoted in "Rethinking Globalization" Year
End-Report, 21st Century Council, December 2017, unpublished (see
http://governance.berggruen.org/meetings/37).

56. Nathan Gardels, "It's a Problem That America Is Still Unable to
Admit It Will Become #2 to China," *The WorldPost,* May 19, 2017,
https://www.huffingtonpost.com/entry/trump-america-first-china-asia_
us_5919fed0e4b0809be15727f5.

57. Lawrence Summers, "How to Embrace Nationalism Responsibly," *Washington Post,* July 10, 2016, https://www.washingtonpost.com
/opinions/global-opinions/how-to-embrace-nationalism-responsibly
/2016/07/10/faf7a100–4507–11e6–8856-f26de2537a9d_story.html?utm_
term=.1554bb0b84e5.

58. Lawrence Summers, "How to Embrace Nationalism Responsibly," *Washington Post,* July 10, 2016, https://www.washingtonpost.com
/opinions/global-opinions/how-to-embrace-nationalism-responsibly
/2016/07/10/faf7a100–4507–11e6–8856-f26de2537a9d_story.html?utm_
term=.6ef101a088f2.

59. Rana Foroohar, "Why America's Tax and Trade Debate Is
Wrong," *Financial Times,* September 24, 2017, https://www.ft.com/content
/aa840e56–9f9d-11e7–8cd4–932067fbf946.

60. "Trump's China Tariffs Would Hit US Firms," *Bloomberg Quint,*
May 16, 2018, https://www.bloombergquint.com/china/2018/05/16
/trump-tariffs-would-tax-u-s-firms-supply-chains-peterson-says.

61. Alexis Crow, "Some German Medicine for Trump," *The World-
Post,* April 11, 2018, https://www.washingtonpost.com/news/theworldpost
/wp/2018/04/11/trump-trade-war/?utm_term=.1e21c807f2d4.

62. Samuel P. Huntington, *Who We Are: The Challenges to America's
National Identity* (New York: Simon and Schuster, 2004), 180.

63. Drew Desilber, "Refugee Surge Brings Youth to an Aging
Europe," Pew Research Center, October 08, 2015, http://www.pewresearch
.org/fact-tank/2015/10/08/refugee-surge-brings-youth-to-an-aging-
europe/; "UNICEF Report: Africa's Population Could Hit 4 Billion by
2100, *Goats and Soda,* National Public Radio, August 13, 2014, http://www

.npr.org/sections/goatsandsoda/2014/08/13/340091377/unicef-report-africas-population-could-hit-4-billion-by-2100.

64. Nathan Gardels, "Two Concepts of Nationalism: An Interview with Isaiah Berlin," *New York Review of Books,* November 12, 1991, http://www.nybooks.com/articles/1991/11/21/two-concepts-of-nationalism-an-interview-with-isai/.

65. Nathan Gardels, "Pankaj Mishra: A Mutiny against Modernizing Elites Has Erupted in the West," *The WorldPost,* February 27, 2017, http://www.huffingtonpost.com/entry/mutiny-modernizing-elites-mishra_us_58b439f8e4b0780bac2b79ad.

66. Nathan Gardels, "The Rise of Europe's Far-Right Is 'a Wake Up Call' for Democracy, Says Turkish Novelist," *The WorldPost,* January 26, 2017, http://www.huffingtonpost.com/entry/europe-far-right-elif-shafak_us_58898c3ee4b0737fd5cb913f?nvlhaor&section=us_world&section=us_world.

67. Kwame Anthony Appiah, *The Lies That Bind: Rethinking Identity* (New York: Liveright, 2018).

68. Nathan Gardels, "Wanting to Preserve Your Way of Life Does Not Make You Racist or Fascist," *The WorldPost,* September 28, 2015, http://www.huffingtonpost.com/nathan-gardels/europe-refugee-rejection_b_8197248.html.

69. Gardels, "Wanting to Preserve Your Way of Life."

70. "The Berggruen Prize," Berggruen Institute, www.berggruen.org/prize.

71. Chris Bloor, "Interview: Charles Taylor," *Philosophy Now* [December 2016], https://philosophynow.org/issues/74/Charles_Taylor.

72. Charles Taylor, *Reconciling the Solitudes: Essays on Canadian Federalism and Nationalism* (Montreal: McGill-Queen's University Press, 1993.

73. "Let's Move On, Says Quebec Accommodation Commission," CBC Montreal, May 22, 2008, http://www.cbc.ca/news/canada/montreal/let-s-move-on-says-quebec-accommodation-commission-1.709976.

74. Paul May, "Why Trump's Plan to Copy Canada's Immigration System Would Backfire," *The WorldPost,* May 1, 2017, http://www

.huffingtonpost.com/entry/trump-immigration-canada_us_58f7bcf2e
4b05b9d613fc639.

75. Richard Milne, "Sweden Tested by Immigration Challenge," *Financial Times,* March 27, 2017, https://www.ft.com/content/838d60c2–0961–11e7–97d1–5e720a26771b.

76. Fabrizio Tassinari, "It's Not All Welfare and Social Justice," *Foreign Affairs,* October 27, 2015, https://www.foreignaffairs.com/articles/northern-europe/2015–10–27/scandinavias-real-lessons.

77. Solberg quoted in Richard Milne, "Nordic Populists Struggle with the Burdens of Power," *Financial Times,* August 10, 2017, https://www.ft.com/content/8443f894–7cf4–11e7–9108-eddaobcbc928

78. Bill Clinton, interview with Nathan Gardels, May 23, 2017, in Year End-Report, 21st Century Council, December 2017.

79. Clinton, interview with Gardels.

80. Bijian, "China's 'One Belt, One Road' Plan Marks the Next Phase of Globalization."

81. Nathan Gardels, "America's Global Influence Depends on Cooperation with China," interview with Zbigniew Brzezinski, *The WorldPost,* December 2016, http://www.huffingtonpost.com/entry/zbigniew-brzezinski-america-influence-china_us_585d8545e4b0d9a594584a37?section=us_world.

82. Kevin Rudd, "How Ancient Chinese Thought Applies Today," *The WorldPost,* February 4, 2015, http://www.huffingtonpost.com/kevin-rudd/chinese-strategic-thoughts_b_6417754.html.

83. Antonio Guterres, "As Refugee Tide Mounts, No One Is in Control," *The WorldPost,* August 27, 2015, http://www.huffingtonpost.com/antanio-guterres/refugee-crisis-control_b_8050468.html?utm_hp_ref=world.

84. Hu Shuli, "Kissinger: China, U.S. 'Must Lead in Cooperation,'" *ChinaFile* (Caixin Media), March 24, 2015, http://www.chinafile.com/reporting-opinion/caixin-media/kissinger-china-us-must-lead-cooperation.

85. Henry Kissinger, interview with authors, October 28, 2014, Century Club, New York.

86. Nathan Gardels, "Is America Ready for China as an 'Equal Brother?'" *The WorldPost,* November 21, 2014, http://www.huffingtonpost

.com/nathan-gardels/henry-kissinger-fu-ying-america-china-discussion_
b_6193804.html.

87. Nick Penzenstadler, "Philippines' Duterte to U.S. Over Aid: 'Bye-bye America,'" *USA Today,* December 17, 2016, https://www .usatoday.com/story/news/world/2016/12/17/philippines-duterte-us-over-aid-bye-bye-america/95557384/.

88. James Steinberg and Michael E. O'Hanlon, *Strategic Reassurance and Resolve: U.S.-China Relations in the Twenty First Century* (Princeton: Princeton University Press, 2014).

89. Henry Kissinger, *World Order* (New York: Penguin Press, 2015), 228.

EPILOGUE

1. Ilya Prigogine, "Beyond Being and Becoming," *New Perspectives Quarterly* (Fall 2004), http://www.digitalnpq.org/archive/2004_fall/01_ prigogine.html.

INDEX